Management for Professionals

The Springer series "Management for Professionals" comprises high-level business and management books for executives, MBA students, and practice-oriented business researchers. The topics cover all themes relevant to businesses and the business ecosystem. The authors are experienced business professionals and renowned professors who combine scientific backgrounds, best practices, and entrepreneurial vision to provide powerful insights into achieving business excellence.

The Series is SCOPUS-indexed.

George Vekinis

The Researcher Entrepreneur

Best Practices for Successful Technological Entrepreneurship

Second Edition

George Vekinis
National Centre for Scientific Research Demokritos
Agia Paraskevi, Greece

ISSN 2192-8096 ISSN 2192-810X (electronic)
Management for Professionals
ISBN 978-3-031-44357-2 ISBN 978-3-031-44358-9 (eBook)
https://doi.org/10.1007/978-3-031-44358-9

1st edition: © The Author 2016

© The Editor(s) (if applicable) and The Author(s), under exclusive license to Springer Nature Switzerland AG 2023
This work is subject to copyright. All rights are solely and exclusively licensed by the Publisher, whether the whole or part of the material is concerned, specifically the rights of translation, reprinting, reuse of illustrations, recitation, broadcasting, reproduction on microfilms or in any other physical way, and transmission or information storage and retrieval, electronic adaptation, computer software, or by similar or dissimilar methodology now known or hereafter developed.
The use of general descriptive names, registered names, trademarks, service marks, etc. in this publication does not imply, even in the absence of a specific statement, that such names are exempt from the relevant protective laws and regulations and therefore free for general use.
The publisher, the authors, and the editors are safe to assume that the advice and information in this book are believed to be true and accurate at the date of publication. Neither the publisher nor the authors or the editors give a warranty, expressed or implied, with respect to the material contained herein or for any errors or omissions that may have been made. The publisher remains neutral with regard to jurisdictional claims in published maps and institutional affiliations.

This Springer imprint is published by the registered company Springer Nature Switzerland AG
The registered company address is: Gewerbestrasse 11, 6330 Cham, Switzerland

Paper in this product is recyclable.

Preface

This book has arisen from the recognition that the process of technology transfer via the setting up of a start-up company, as introduced in my previous book, [1] frequently comes to a stop or breaks down not because of any particular innate difficulties associated with the new technology but mainly because commercialisation of results (or "exploitation", as it is often called) requires a rather different set of skills and mindset to those needed to conduct good research. This recognition is often not readily obvious to (or appreciated by) researchers and inventors and is particularly evident in the case of researchers attempting the jump to entrepreneurship without adequate preparation. And yet, a good researcher has, potentially, many of the skills needed for good entrepreneurship.

In the previous book, I made a point of (almost) discouraging researchers and inventors from attempting to proceed with the technology transfer (TT) process through their own venture (i.e. a start-up company) as their preferred first course of action. Instead, I argued that they should opt for a collaboration with an existing healthy company which, by virtue of its good standing in its markets, will be in a better position to get the new technology accepted by users. Such collaboration, if possible and if it comes to pass, offers many potential benefits, not least of which is the financial and engineering backing necessary during this crucial early period as well as readily available capability for comparative pilot and field testing.

It remains a fact, however, that this route is not at all easy to follow or to get just right. A large majority of researchers and inventors who attempt technology transfer often feel that they are banging on closed doors and that the "obvious" benefits and competitiveness that their new technology offers (at least, "obvious" as they themselves perceive them) are not appreciated or recognised by potential users. Over time, many become so frustrated by the constant rebuffs and obstacles they encounter that they eventually consider giving up and withdrawing back into the safe haven

---

[1] "Mastering Technology Transfer: from invention to innovation. A step-by-step guide for Researchers and Inventors", George Vekinis, Springer, 2023. Referred to in this book as "TT Guide".

of their laboratories. This is obviously something which every country tries to avoid; utilisable research results should always find their way to the market or society.

My premise in this book therefore is that, once they have attempted technology transfer via licensing or co-development unsuccessfully, researchers and inventors whose technology is well proven should consider the alternative commercialisation route of *going it alone*, either by setting up a new start-up company or by spinning off one from a university, research centre, or an existing company. After all, if some researchers and inventors have succeeded in establishing and leading successful start-ups, why not others too?

It is this group of researchers and inventors – we may call them *researcher entrepreneurs* – who this book is aimed at. It is true that the difficulties inherent in such a venture are formidable – as attested by the small number of successful technological start-ups. Yet, it is also true that with sufficient support and knowledge of the crucial "dos and don'ts of entrepreneurship" as well as plenty of patience and perseverance, your efforts can pay off handsomely and your own start-up can become one of the success stories.

This book does not purport to offer all the answers. And it is not meant to be a detailed guide on how to prepare, build and run a start-up company. Many good books exist with detailed information and advice on how to set up a start-up company and how to manage the many facets of its operation, from personnel to marketing and sales.

What this book *does* is to consider and discuss many of the *critical aspects* and *questions* that arise both during the preparatory phases and during the early operation of your start-up. Over the course of many years, I have had the opportunity to witness and study the birth and development of a large number of start-up companies, many of which were spun off from research laboratories in an attempt to commercialise research results. As a result, many common misconceptions have become apparent to me, especially on the part of researchers, which seem to crop up time and time again during attempts to set up a start-up. It is these misconceptions and false leads that so often lead to abortive attempts to commercialise otherwise very promising technologies, and it is these which I have tried to clarify in this book. As is so often the case, it is the failures that teach us most of the lessons connected with entrepreneurship. Whether a start-up fails early or late in its (often short) life, such case studies are particularly instructive and therefore many of the chapters in this book draw on real cases that I have had the opportunity to study closely and often be associated with.

In an attempt at brevity, I have deliberately kept the chapters short so as to focus on the most critical aspects that can undermine or facilitate the researcher-entrepreneur's efforts in his or her efforts to leave the lab and become an entrepreneur.

Perhaps you are reading this book to help you make up your mind, or perhaps you are already convinced to "go it alone" and industrialise or commercialise your brainchild via a start-up or a spin-off company. Whatever your motive, I sincerely hope that you will enjoy reading it as much as I enjoyed writing it and that it will help you on your journey to entrepreneurial success!

Agia Paraskevi, Greece
July 2023

George Vekinis

The original version of this book was revised, and the author biography has been included in the front matter of the book on Page xi.

Contents

1	Researchers and Entrepreneurship	1
2	Bridging Two Worlds	9
3	Nothing Ventured, Nothing Gained	13
4	Decisions, Decisions	19
5	An Invention Is not an Innovation	25
6	Opportunities Are Everywhere... and if There Aren't, Create Them!	29
7	Can You Manage as well as You Research?	35
8	Strong Foundations	39
9	Aim for Perfection	43
10	Strategise like a 5* General	47
11	There Is More than One Way to Rome	53
12	Be Disruptive... But Don't Disrupt!	57
13	Think Ahead and Fit the Purpose	61
14	Is Your Financial Base Solid?	65
15	In... Agreements We Trust	71
16	Timing Is Critical	75
17	Risk Wisely	81
18	Protect Your Technology... But Not Too Much!	87
19	Viability, Not Just Feasibility	91
20	Skilling and Re-skilling	95
21	The Market Is Your Guide	99
22	Position, Position, Position	103

23	Commercialisation Readiness Index	107
24	Obstacles Are Just Challenges	113
25	There Is Always That Little Bit Extra You Can Offer	119
26	Consolidate First, Diversify Later	125
27	Diamonds from Ashes	129
28	Open a Window to the World	135
29	A Final Thought: Proactivity Beats Reactivity Every Time	139

Further Reading 143

About the Author

Dr. George Vekinis is Director of Research at the National Research Centre "Demokritos" (NCSRD) in Greece. In the past, he served as Director of the Education Office of NCSRD, President of the Researchers' Association, President of the Hellenic Society of Condensed Matter and in numerous scientific committees of various conferences. In the past, he worked as a Chief Researcher at the Council for Scientific and Industrial Research in South Africa and as an associate researcher at the Engineering Department of the University of Cambridge, UK. He is currently teaching post graduate courses in Innovation Management at the Technical University of Crete and in Advanced Materials at the Aristotelian University of Thessaloniki. In the past, he was a visiting professor and speaker to many institutions in Europe, Asia, and the USA, a senior consultant in Technology Transfer and Entrepreneurship for the European Commission and a reviewer and impact assessor of many international research projects. He is the President of AIT SA and has mentored a number of start-up companies. He has published nearly 300 publications, reports, and conference presentations, two monographs on technology transfer and entrepreneurship and a popular science book entitled "Physics in the kitchen."

List of Figures

Fig. 1.1	A simplified flowchart of the *research process* which by Stage 8 produces a range of feasible solutions to a need or phenomenon.	2
Fig. 1.2	A simplified flowchart of the *technological entrepreneurship process* via a start-up company. Many details have been omitted for clarity.	4
Fig. 2.1	The research world is bridged to the business world of the start-up via many critical activities and checks which help to ensure successful technology transfer. These correspond to the activities in Stages 4–8 of the TT process as discussed in the TT Guide.	10
Fig. 6.1	Breakthroughs, instabilities, or imbalances are all fertile grounds for new technological enterprises.	31
Fig. 8.1	The quality and completeness of the foundation pillars are critical for the success of the enterprise.	40
Fig. 9.1	All links in the development and commercialisation chain must be as strong as possible to ensure the integrity of the whole chain.	45
Fig. 12.1	(**a**) A new process (or device, material, etc.) may be used in parallel with an existing process and gradually replace the existing process. No disruption to operations required. (**b**) A new process may be included in the production as an assisting process, increasing efficiency and eventually replacing the existing process. No or minimal disruption to operations required.	58
Fig. 14.1	Various funding sources available for start-ups and associated issues.	68
Fig. 17.1	The main categories of risk for technology commercialisation via a start-up company. For more details and SWOT analysis and strategies for analysing, predicting, and handling risk, see the TT Guide.	84

Fig. 22.1　Six market positioning dimensions with illustrative examples for three generic technologies: M, advanced material; CG, computer game; S, sensor; VAR, value-added reseller; OEM, original equipment manufacturer 104

Fig. 25.1　Functional convergence analysis to identify potential alternative areas of application of your technology 121

List of Tables

Table 23.1	A scoring matrix to determine your aggregate Commercialisation Readiness Index (CRI) (scores shown refer to a real case)	108
Table 23.2	The CRI matrix of the case study in Table 23.1 after improvements in design and prototype production ideas	110
Table 24.1	The main sources of operational problems and their main repercussions during the early life of a start-up	114
Table 26.1	A scoring system for deciding the most optimum debut market for your technology. Use zero (0) for "Nothing" and "5" for "Maximum". Scores shown refer to a real case, as discussed in the text	127
Table 27.1	Common reasons for failure of a technology commercialisation attempt and possible responses for remediation	132
Table 28.1	Suggested technology information dissemination channels according to type of technology	136

Researchers and Entrepreneurship

Entrepreneurship or entrepreneurial spirit can be defined as "the capacity and willingness to develop, organize and manage a business venture, along with any of its risks, in order to make a profit"[1].

The underlying point here is that an entrepreneur needs specific skills ("capacity") but also the commitment ("willingness") to take the steps necessary to set up and run a start-up company successfully. Are these capabilities really so rare in academia and research that few researchers are able to take up the challenge of setting up an enterprise to transform their research results into an innovative product or service?

Commitment of course stems mainly from one's desire to succeed and is indeed common both to the research and to the business environments. On the other hand, so the oft-quoted wisdom goes, the "entrepreneurial skills required for successful entrepreneurship are very different from what good researchers have". Is this actually true? I think the truth is far from it. I believe that any good, committed, scientific researcher has both the capacity and most of the critical skills necessary to become a good entrepreneur. What is needed is a different outlook!

Let's consider and compare the two worlds. Scientific researchers are generally trained to apply the so-called scientific method which can be summarised as follows: Query→ Analyse → Theorise →Design → Test → Analyse → Repeat until satisfied.

With time, this method of carrying out research becomes second nature to all researchers, and we carry out all our research work along these lines with only rare deviations. The flowchart in Fig. 1.1 illustrates this quite simply.

The basic stages are always the same. We start by responding to a need (a demand or a request, etc.) or an observation or a phenomenon. The response is usually in terms of a query: "Why?", which is then formulated in such a way so as to allow the analytical development of a number of possible answers or solutions.

---

[1] BusinessDictionary.com (2016).

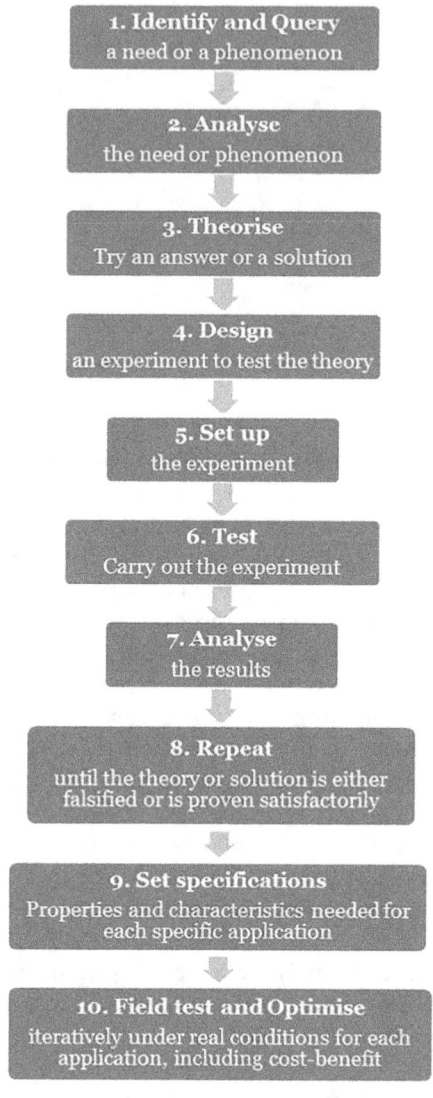

Fig. 1.1 A simplified flowchart of the *research process* which by Stage 8 produces a range of feasible solutions to a need or phenomenon

In the next stages, each potential solution is tested and the results analysed to check if they offer a satisfactory answer to the original need or phenomenon. This is the "proof of concept" stage and offers a measure of the technical feasibility of each solution. This process is repeated (Stage 8 in Fig. 1.1) for all potential (theoretical) answers or solutions, and this is usually the stage where most research efforts are completed.

Generally, this process does not produce a specific competitive product or service. More often than not, it results in a range of feasible solutions especially since, by and large, a number of researchers study the same need or phenomenon independently and usually arrive at different solutions. These solutions are all at a Technology Readiness Level[2] (TRL) of approximately 4.

If, however, an "optimum" solution is required, e.g., a competitive product, process, or service which must abide by a set of specifications, then the research process continues with the feasible solutions found in Stage 8 being critically assessed and iteratively developed further, under real conditions. After taking into account cost-benefit considerations, indicated in Stage 10 of Fig. 1.1, an optimum "viable" technological solution is arrived at for each specific application which is now at TRL7-8.

This is the solution – a material, a product, a process, a method, a service, etc. – that will generally be the subject of a technology transfer process and perhaps lead to its commercialisation. It will be the main subject and asset of the start-up business venture where it will be developed further industrially and eventually offered to the market.

The above account is a simplified version of the research and development process which feeds into the TT process. A much more detailed discussion is provided in the TT Guide, and I recommend you to read through at least the information and summary boxes in that book for a more extensive account and more comprehensive information regarding many aspects of the TT process.

Entrepreneurship

So how does the research process, described in the above flowchart, compare with the business process, especially as regards technological entrepreneurship? Perhaps surprisingly, the two processes have many similarities. As we'll see, many of the stages (and skills!) required are very similar in both worlds; in fact, many of the skills that researchers have are (almost) directly applicable and valuable in a start-up enterprise.

The flowchart in Fig. 1.2 shows a flowchart of the main stages of technological entrepreneurship. Considering the details, it becomes apparent that the similarities are several and quite remarkable. Let's consider each stage in turn.

All business ventures address a need or a demand which is seen as an "opportunity" to serve society, to make a profit, or both. This means that the business process always starts by identifying such opportunities before anybody else does and finding a good solution to address that need or demand.

Business opportunities are literally everywhere and the mark of an astute entrepreneur is his or her ability to identify them quickly and profitably. A huge number of examples exist in our own time: from the identification of the need for easy social interaction with people beyond our immediate circle which led to the now ubiquitous online social networking and instant communication services such as Linked-In, Facebook, and Twitter to mobile telephony, a plethora of apps for smart phones, etc.

---

[2]For a detailed discussion of TRLs, see the TT Guide.

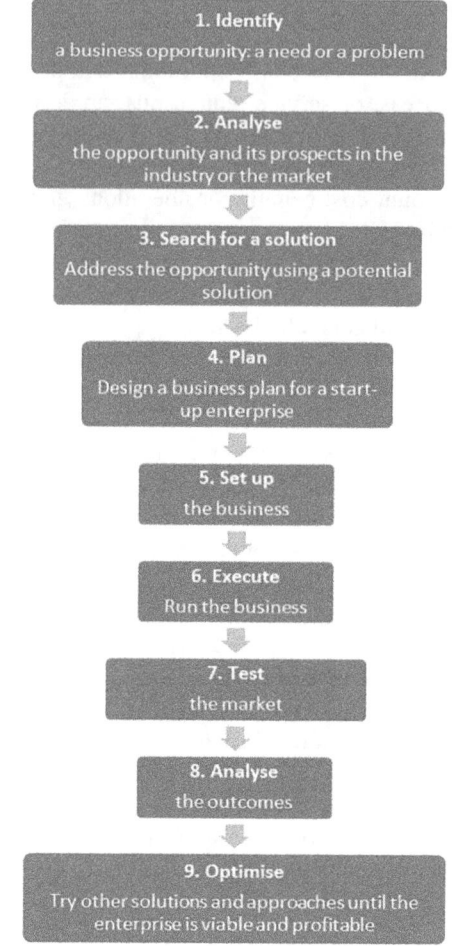

Fig. 1.2 A simplified flowchart of the *technological entrepreneurship process* via a start-up company. Many details have been omitted for clarity

In fact, many new start-ups are founded everyday based on someone's idea for addressing a need or a demand, however ephemeral it might turn out to be. Such ideas are not always purely functional of course – witness the myriad computer games that now form a huge global entertainment industry.

To evaluate whether the identified idea is indeed novel and potentially profitable, the identification stage is always followed by a critical analysis of the opportunity vis-à-vis its market or industry potential. At this stage, the optimum solution may not have been identified yet, in which case a search needs to be made for a ready solution or a project initiated to develop a solution, sometimes with the help of a research organisation. In the case of technology transfer, we are now at the end of the research process, i.e. Stage 10 in Fig. 1.1, and ready to launch our start-up company.

It is at this point, when the whole picture is clearer, that a business plan is prepared and put into action. We'll consider some of the aspects of the business plan (and the dos and don'ts of a good plan) in later chapters, but at the moment, all we need to stress is that the success of the whole business venture depends always on the *quality* of the business plan and its *reliable implementation*. It is not enough for an opportunity to be identified – you also need to have the solution (or at least the *potential* solution) carefully thought out and primed so as to "fit" the opportunity.

Assuming that funding has been secured, the first step of the implementation of the business plan is to set up the start-up company. This could be completely independent or it could be connected to an existing establishment. In the latter case, this is called a "spin-off" company. If the solution has not yet been fully developed, it is the company's main objective to develop or adapt the potential solution for the specific opportunity identified.

As soon as the solution has been developed and tested exhaustively to a final shape and functionality, it can be introduced to the market (or markets), something which is usually done gradually in a first version. The results are analysed and through an iterative process the solution is optimised for the particular market.

A Meeting of Skills

The above discussion of the research and the entrepreneurial processes makes it clear that many of the basic skills are common to both worlds. Both research and entrepreneurship rely on analytical capabilities to evaluate both the opportunities and the solutions, to couple them effectively and profitably and to optimise the solution iteratively.

Most importantly, both good researchers and good entrepreneurs *take the initiative* and are good *innovators*. The former are technology innovators, whereas the latter are technological business innovators. The former sharpen the solution, whereas the latter are good at finding the way to couple it with the identified opportunity. The level of innovativeness in both worlds is the same, but the *outlook* and *viewpoint* are different: researchers prepare the inventions which are then taken over by entrepreneurs to turn them into valuable innovations. The aim of this book is to show that it is possible to combine the two into one person: the Researcher Entrepreneur!

Even at a closer level of inspection, many similarities are evident. The search for a solution to address an opportunity is very similar to the searches (and the related methodology) that researchers undertake in order to solve a particular problem in their laboratories. They both involve prior knowledge and experience, and both very often rely on trial and error to reach a promising answer.

And at the analysis stages, both researchers and entrepreneurs analyse and correlate the tests carried out with the results, and very often the statistical tools used are identical. Both are able to perceive quickly when something is not working out which is their signal to go back to the drawing board.

In summary, successful researchers and successful entrepreneurs are both characterised by their capability and willingness on the following:

- Take the initiative.
- Identify opportunities and go after them.
- Be able to analyse situations and take decisions.
- Follow through with decisions and adjust as necessary.
- Have patience and perseverance.
- Be flexible.
- Develop a vision and a clear aim.
- Not be easily disappointed.
- Bounce back after temporary setbacks with new ideas and approaches.

A New Set of Skills

So if researchers possess so many of the *technical* skills necessary for successful entrepreneurship, why do so many of them balk at the attempt to transfer their technology via a start-up? And of those enterprises that are set up by researchers in order to exploit a new technology, why do so few succeed in the long term?

The reasons are complex and we'll examine most – if not all – of them in this book. If we take it for granted that the technology is indeed developed to a suitably advanced technical level and is technically competitive (aspects which I have discussed in the TT Guide), then I believe the main reasons for the difficulties encountered by start-ups are non-technical and that many are connected to the innately different approaches we take in research and in entrepreneurship.

I am referring to the non-technical skills that are required for successful entrepreneurship, *few of which are needed or developed in a research environment.* Mainly, these concern the ability to take decisions quickly without clear knowledge of all the facts, to identify and manage non-technical risks, and to be able to "stand back" and look critically at one's own technology from the eyes of a potential user, concentrating on its *relative value* and apparent utility under the conditions in which it could be used. Here, the difference between the skill sets of the researcher and the entrepreneur becomes apparent, and it is in this encounter with the world of entrepreneurship that the researcher's skills and tools alone cannot get him or her very far. How, then, is one to navigate one's transformation into this necessary hybrid: the Researcher Entrepreneur?

It actually turns out to be easier than most people expect. All we need are some tools to bridge the two worlds and the presence of mind to apply them in such a way as to maximise the skills one has as a researcher. These will form the focus of the following chapters.

In Summary

There are few similarities between the scientific process and thetechnological entrepreneurship process. Both involve systematic searching for optimum solutions via iterations and both often rely on trial and error. But in the former case, research is mostly open-ended (we don't always know what we'll find), whereas in the second case, we aim for a specific product or service. A researcher and an entrepreneur also require different skill sets, but it is not impossible for a researcher to learn to become a Researcher Entrepreneur.

Bridging Two Worlds 2

The decision to set up a start-up company is essentially a decision to bridge two worlds: the world of the research laboratory where the invention is nurtured and developed and the world of business where the technology (now in the form of a valuable innovation) must prove itself and be accepted by the market. While the former is characterised by well-controlled conditions and carefully planned developments, the latter is characterised by external influences and externally set conditions which one cannot normally change or influence.

The technology transfer process is fraught with difficulties and unknowns. The conversion of a novel technology to a product or tool or service, etc. is certainly a very difficult task, and few technologies succeed in actually reaching the other side. The level of difficulty springs not only from the fact that running a start-up requires a completely different way of thinking but also because success depends on many factors that are very often beyond our control.

This is why *planning and preparation* are so important and *risk management* at all stages is so crucial.

Preparation of the technology for the transition from the lab to the start-up involves many activities (all of which are discussed in detail in the TT Guide) which take place during Stages 4–8 of the technology transfer process.[1] Some of the most important activities are shown in the centre bridge of the schematic diagram in Fig. 2.1.

In the research world on the left, the technology is tested and optimised until its properties and functionality conform to the original design (assuming the technology was produced "to order") and the expected usage and interoperability. In other words, it is here that the *technical feasibility* of the technology for a specific application is confirmed.

---

[1] See the TT Guide for description of the stages of the transformation of an invention to an innovation.

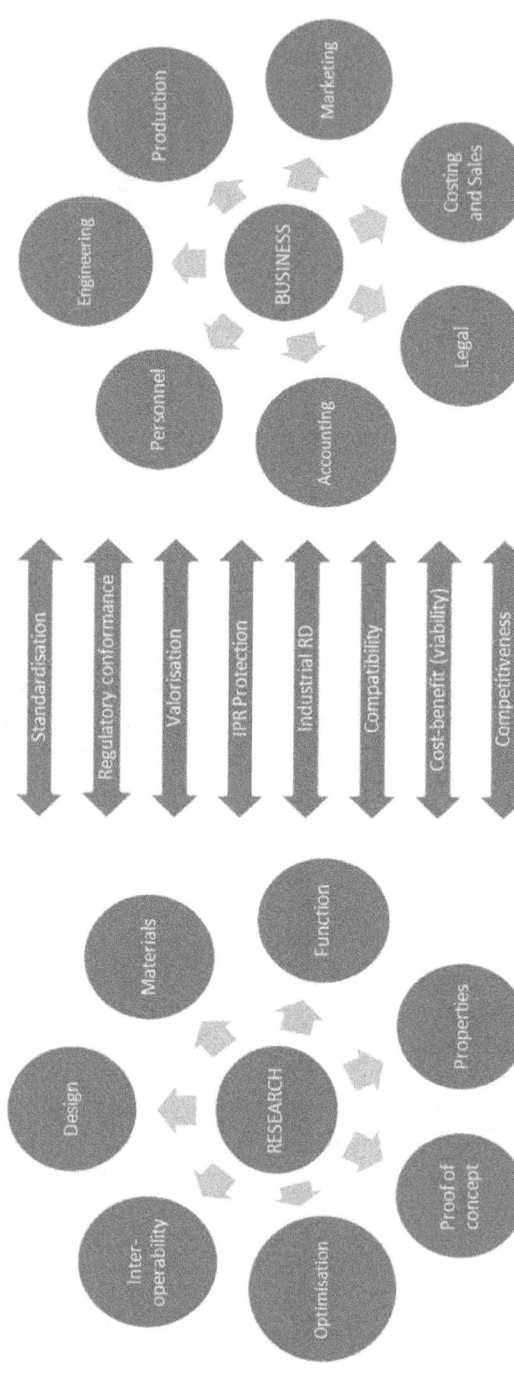

Fig. 2.1 The research world is bridged to the business world of the start-up via many critical activities and checks which help to ensure successful technology transfer. These correspond to the activities in Stages 4–8 of the TT process as discussed in the TT Guide

However, in order to enable the transition to the business world (i.e. the Invention → Innovation transformation), the technology needs to be further suitably developed and enhanced so as to be acceptable and competitive in the target market. In particular, it needs to be protected (formally, e.g. by patenting, and/or informally, e.g. by keeping it secret) and checked for compatibility with the systems it will work with or be installed in and also for conformance with any standards and regulations. It must also be valorised (i.e. improve its relative value) and optimised as much as possible with respect to what the market needs or demands.

Most importantly, the new technology has to display clear *viability* in its chosen application or market. Its cost-benefit ratio must be such that its competitiveness with respect to other technologies (existing or potential) for this application is *clear* and *satisfactory*. In particular, if the technology is aimed at replacing an existing technology which is already well established, then it will need to demonstrate particularly high cost competitiveness, taking into account the necessary costs for any (necessary) adjustments, retooling, or re-engineering and any new investment costs as well. One must also keep in mind that all industries and markets are cyclical in their operations and a new technology must be carefully timed to coincide with the period when new investments or purchases are planned if it is to have any chance of being accepted.

Bridging of the two worlds should be done gradually and carefully. A "pilot" stage is always essential where scaling up is carried out and the technology is adjusted so that it responds to actual users' needs and usage. Many customer-oriented technologies (especially software) undergo extensive controlled testing called "alpha-testing" where knowledgeable users from inside the company (or chosen by the company) are encouraged to use it under various conditions in order to pick-out potential problems or "bugs". After a period during which many problems are resolved, the technology is released in the open market where "beta-testing" is carried out by as wide a spectrum of users as possible and where further problems may appear which can be ironed out before final market release.

In Summary

Bridging the lab and the market is not straightforward and requires systematic and methodical work to transform an invention to an innovative product or service. Commercialisation via a start-up is the most difficult route but offers independence and relative rapidity, and eventual success can bring many concrete and major benefits to a researcher entrepreneur.

Nothing Ventured, Nothing Gained   3

While there is never a guarantee of success in setting up a start-up for the commercialisation of your technology, doing nothing and sitting in your lab is certainly not the way to bring it to industry or the market. As the owner of the technology, commercialisation is entirely up to you and you will only stand a chance of gaining benefits from your efforts if you act – nobody else will do it for you.

As researchers, we learn to be doubtful of unusual results and extra careful when we check our measurements, especially when we announce them – at least, so we should be. The decision to become an entrepreneur should be dictated by the same principles of caution and preparedness. In contrast to an experienced entrepreneur, however, many lab researchers tend to be put off entrepreneurship by their over-cautious fear of the "unknown" and do not take the plunge due to their (understandable) doubt regarding the likelihood of eventual success after a lot of effort. In all cases of course, good preparation and good management will maximise the chances for success and reduce problems; everything, however, starts with the first step, i.e. the *decision* to set up a start-up for commercialisation.

And it is this first step that is the most difficult to take. Having a permanent research or academic position means job security and a very low incentive to try something which will invariably reduce the time you can spend in the lab or writing papers (necessary for academics' and researchers' promotion [1]). This is the main reason why the Researcher Entrepreneur is such a rare person, although it should not be so! The true pity here is that a great number of very worthwhile technologies developed by researchers remain uncommercialised and never get utilised. Many never even see the light of day beyond the lab – the sad thing is that so many are forgotten and often have to be re-invented when the need arises. The need to continuously compete for funding grants also means that promising technologies

---

[1] Personally I find this "publish or perish" pressure on academics and researchers extremely counter-productive. We are forced to spend most of our time writing publications or grant proposals instead of developing technologies and transforming them into useful products.

cannot be developed well beyond the time horizon of the grant itself as the researcher is forced to jump to the next grant and to the next technology just to stay afloat.

Look around you in your lab. You will surely find a number of technologies sitting around your lab which have never found their way to an industrial application or a market. Or they may have been published and then promptly picked up and commercialised by third parties. Wouldn't it have been more satisfactory and profitable if you had commercialised them yourself and benefited from your own efforts?

There are many ways for a researcher to commercialise a technology or know-how, assuming that it does address a need or demand on the part of a user or market. There is at least one way, among many, of commercialising your technology (or technologies) which will be ideal in your particular case and which will bring you direct benefits, if only you take the plunge. On one end of the scale, you can offer advice or consulting to help a user adopt the technology, all the way to the other end of the scale where you can set up your own start-up to produce it and sell it directly. A plethora of intermediate routes includes a whole range of technology transfer activities such as licensing or outright selling the rights, a joint venture with a producer or user, and many others. Not all technologies are amenable to all of these commercialisation routes, of course. For example, a unique sensor that addresses a niche need (e.g. in space exploration) would find it an uphill battle to find a producer to license it or produce it and the only reasonable commercialisation route may be a start-up company, assuming that the market research shows sufficient financial returns to make it worthwhile. In other cases, the opposite is true. For example, a product that is an evolved version of one already existing in the market would more easily be accepted via a joint venture or licensing agreement with the producer of the existing product.

In all cases, commercialisation always begins with the decision to transfer your technology to a commercial entity, a decision which is not always easy to make if you are a laboratory researcher. Although you probably can see (and perhaps even dream of) the benefits, the realisation that you will need to sacrifice much of your time and consequently reduce your research efforts in order to succeed as an entrepreneur is a major brake to entrepreneurship. You have probably been told that to succeed as an entrepreneur you will need to give 100% of your time and efforts – which in many cases is close to the truth – which means precious little time left to do your research. Is there any way out of this impasse? Is there any way to balance the lives of a researcher and an entrepreneur in such a way as to have – as close as possible – the best of both worlds?

I believe the answer is "probably". By directing your commercialisation efforts in just the right way and with just the right amount of energy – no more and no less – you could have substantial free time for your research and allow you to balance both of your working lives. Many people have managed this very well, and somewhat surprisingly, this can be easier to achieve if commercialisation is carried out via a start-up (or spin-off) rather than via alternative routes such as a joint venture or licensing out.

The secret lies in the fact that in a start-up it is much easier to control several aspects of the commercialisation process and decision-making is much quicker. First, you have control over the amount of time you personally have to spend guiding the company. Second, you have control over the very important decisions regarding which secret technological aspects of your technology are critical enough that they need to be kept under wraps and which should only be disclosed for strategic reasons. Third, in setting up your own start-up company, you are free to take all strategic decisions yourself – this includes ways in which you can balance your research and entrepreneurship activities. All of these things are nearly impossible if you are in a joint venture or if you license out your technology.

To illustrate this, let us consider a frequently encountered technological example (based on a real case I have encountered): you've come across an unusual way to improve the properties (e.g. the thermal stability and performance) of an existing material used for large-scale applications (e.g. for photo-voltaic solar panels). The secret lies in some new ingredient (applied by some standard additive process on a substrate) which has taken you much effort to discover, but which is rather obvious in retrospect. How do you protect and then commercialise such a research finding? We shall discuss the secrets of effective protection later on, but for now, let us consider how you can have the best of both worlds – that is, how can you commercialise this new and valuable discovery while continuing to work as a researcher?

The answer in this case is simply to concentrate your start-up's activities on producing only the new (secret) ingredient which you will sell to the manufacturers of the large-scale application as a proprietary additive under a contracted "license to use". As long as the performance improvement is satisfactory, the manufacturer will be happy to use it and will not attempt to reverse-engineer your additive, especially if your agreement contains strict penalties for any attempt at infringement. This is the route favoured by many discoverers of catalysts, new micro-alloyed metals and other materials and chemicals. Having proceeded with such a commercialisation route for your start-up, you can happily continue your research in parallel and develop further enhancements of your material. By keeping the end user notified of and satisfied with new developments, they will happily continue the business collaboration. In other words, this route will give you the very valuable freedom both to commercialise and to research.

There are other types of commercialisation routes that can offer similar freedom to commercialise while you continue your research, thereby eliminating the either/or conundrum as to whether you should remain a researcher or become an entrepreneur. It is perfectly possible to combine the two, and an example may help to clarify this further.

Recently, I was involved in a commercialisation process for a new, unique sensor developed for monitoring, in real time, the wear of the inner protective refractory layers used in furnaces, kilns, boilers, etc. Because of the aggressive environments involved, no other in situ sensors appear to exist up to this time, and decisions regarding replacement or re-building of the refractory are generally taken based only on previous experience. Nevertheless, users of such furnaces or boilers would like to know the exact condition of their refractory linings since any damage can have serious consequences, least of which being energy wastage. To protect the sensor, a patent application has been submitted without disclosing the detailed design secret which ensures high reliability and performance. The obvious commercialisation route in this case was to set up a spin-off company which outsources the production of the main body of the sensor which is then simply sealed, connected to the electronics, and supplied to users. For strategic purposes, the spin-off signed agreements with companies that specialise in rebuilding refractory layers and do the actual retrofitting of the sensors in the furnaces. All the spin-off is doing is designing and carrying out additional testing and selling of externally manufactured sensors. Such commercialisation decisions have allowed the researcher who developed the sensor to keep his involvement in the company to a minimum, giving him the freedom to continue the research and development of the sensor for other applications and in other sectors, notably space, critical road surfaces, brake pads, etc.

By planning and acting along such lines, you will soon discover – like many researcher entrepreneurs have over the years – that decisions regarding commercialisation will become easier and more satisfactory while you will remain free to continue your work as a researcher.

There is a saying that encapsulates much of the spirit of the research community: "once a researcher, always a researcher". An engineer or physicist or chemist or biologist or geneticist or whoever has trained as a researcher will always wonder, test, observe with a healthy dose of doubt, and critically analyse his or her results in the hope of discovering something new and significant. It becomes part of our way of thinking and even second nature. So it is perfectly natural that we would like to remain in the lab, where we are most comfortable and where we can indulge in our research for the sake of research. This has led naturally to very high knowledge productivity and the current flood of publications and announcements. But have all these publications actually benefitted humanity to the degree expected?

Actual technological progress – with both social and financial benefits – only became a reality once research was formalised and rightly recognised as the critical bridge between knowledge and industry. It could therefore certainly be argued that public researchers have a responsibility to commercialise their technologies so that society can benefit and progress in sustainable and forward-looking ways. Much of our technological civilisation would not have been achieved if researchers in the past had not ventured into the unknown territory of entrepreneurship, gaining much along the way not only for themselves but for society as a whole. Extending our activities into the entrepreneurial world for the benefit of society is not just a privilege but also a way to reciprocate what society has offered us. All we need to do is take the first step.

In Summary

Many researchers and academics find the commercialisation process daunting and challenging at best. The unfortunate pressure which most institutions place on them to "publish or perish" means that there is generally not enough motivation to attempt commercialisation of even very promising technologies. The end result is that potentially valuable innovations are lost or commercialised by third parties and the inventor derives minimal benefit. Only by venturing out of their comfort zone can a researcher derive maximum profit from their ideas and inventions.

4. Decisions, Decisions

The online Business Dictionary defines an entrepreneur as "someone who exercises initiative by organizing a venture to take benefit of an opportunity and, as the decision-maker, decides what, how, and how much of a good or service will be produced".

The operative word here is "decision-maker". As the well-known American phrase goes, the "buck stops here", i.e. all main decisions in a start-up company have to be made by the entrepreneur. And they always have to shoulder the full *responsibility* for their decisions. This is management at its most difficult since there is no one "above" you to direct you or guide you.

Of course, this level of responsibility is not unique to enterprises; a director of a research laboratory is often in a similar position, albeit with fewer repercussions on the future of the laboratory and certainly fewer responsibilities. A crucial difference may be noted between the lab and enterprise situations: while there may be many facts about particular situations and events that often are not immediately available during the running of a company, decisions related to these factors still must be made without undue delay and consequences faced and addressed. In the enterprise situation, delays or wrong decisions may be very costly and nearly all business decisions have repercussions for the future of the company. An experienced entrepreneur may take such decisions on the basis of hunches and calculated risks rather than clear knowledge of a situation, knowing that there is a chance that he or she may have to take corrective action at a later stage. This is all part of running a company and it cannot be avoided. Suffice to say, this is certainly not how research is carried out. If a researcher aims to become an entrepreneur, he or she needs to go beyond the certainties that underpin research decisions and learn to take decisions under conditions in which not all facts are known. At the same time, they need to develop methods and a mindset which allows for fast decision taking, very much unlike most research which allows for some time complacency. In other words, the researcher needs to exit his or her comfort zone and learn to manage *risks* and be adaptive every step of the way.

Of course, the researcher also has to take decisions in areas which are not directly related to his or her work but which can affect the future development of the new technology nevertheless. A non-exhaustive list would include the following:

- Feasibility of scientific concept
- Design and analysis of experiments
- Technical design of device, system, etc.
- Technical application targeting
- Prototyping and pre-engineering
- Compatibility and interoperability conformance
- Technical risk analysis and management
- Proof of concept
- Protection
- Preliminary cost-benefit analysis
- Regulatory conformity
- And more

A researcher's life in the lab is relatively stress-free, at least in this regard. Most decisions related to their research only have to be made once the scientific or technological facts are known and explored. This makes for accurate scientific decisions of course and so it should be. Although all experienced researchers also work with hunches and "educated" guesses to point new ways forward, they will not take a decision until the experimental facts are on the table and well analysed.

This is one of the main differences between running a laboratory and running a company and one of the biggest changes that researchers have to make towards becoming entrepreneurs. The difference is one of *outlook* and *approach*, and it is this that most characterises the challenging transition from becoming a researcher to a researcher entrepreneur. It's certainly not an easy change to manage as it requires a different outlook and approach to life.

Let's consider an example I encountered some years ago: an entrepreneur has spent a lot of money developing a particular industrial device through his start-up company, but before the device can be released to the market, the market has shifted to a different approach and practice – this happens often. What can the entrepreneur do in this case? There are a number of alternatives: push ahead regardless and find new markets; change direction; change technology; etc. However, few facts are known about any of these. Because of time pressure, a decision had to be made quickly. In this instance, they decided to push ahead and offer it to new, less ideal markets. It was risky and only partially succeeded. At a later stage, the device was re-engineered and an attempt is now under way to enter the main market. The last news I have is that the venture is eventually succeeding.

It is clear therefore that business decisions are often based on hunches and indications rather than actual facts. They are often based on the psychology of the market and the customers, on current economic conditions and trends, and on many other external factors. An entrepreneur needs to be in touch with the markets and sensitive to trends, market responses, and economy-wide changes. A non-exhaustive

4 Decisions, Decisions 21

list of areas where an entrepreneur would have to take decisions based on hunches includes the following:

- Production process design and installations
- Comparative costing to ensure viability
- Sales and marketing strategy
- Market targeting and strategy
- Personnel and skills strategy
- Non-technical risk analysis and management
- Process and market prioritisation
- Legal and contractual aspects
- Conflict resolution
- Sourcing and security of supply
- Strategic alliances and networks
- Countrywide restrictions and constrains
- And more

Another example relates to Intellectual Property Rights (IPR). A device (a chemical sensor) is being developed by a start-up company which owns the IPR and has applied for a patent. The national patent has been granted, but the search results from the European Patent Office (EPO) show a potential conflict with a claim in a national patent in another European country, granted more than 5 years before. In order to circumvent the conflict, a technical change is made to the patent application which is resubmitted to the EPO. A decision must now be made quickly: should this change be incorporated in the new technology, which will mean a delay and greater cost, or should the technology be completed and marketed in Europe as is, avoiding only the country where the IPR conflict exists? Both approaches are legal, but the answer will be different according to which advisor you ask, so the final decision is in the entrepreneur's hands. In this instance, it was decided to incorporate the change in the sensor, even though it delayed market entry and increased costs by at least 25%, all because of the paramount importance of the market. Will it succeed? Only time will tell, but at the moment it is very promising.

These are the type of decisions that a technology entrepreneur might come across as well as many others related to the day-to-day running of the company, to personnel, to funding, to relative cost-benefit of raw materials, etc. The majority of researchers rarely have to deal with management questions relating to local authorities and regulations, personnel, or taxation. These are all things, however, that entrepreneurs have to deal with as a matter of course – indeed, frequently, as a matter of urgency. When a market suddenly refuses to accept one's products because of a sudden shift in expectations (perhaps due to another new product which appears to be more competitive), the entrepreneur must be able to take a decision quickly and accurately: should a completely new market be found or should the product be re-engineered in an attempt to satisfy the new market position? Should the price be dropped temporarily, or should the production cost be reduced, even if this risks reducing the quality?

Having (or acquiring) the capability to organise and run a new venture in an effort to transfer your technology is above all a management challenge. But an entrepreneur needs to be able to do more than just manage. A researcher entrepreneur is a *visionary* with a mission, and he or she needs to lead and to convince others to follow if the new enterprise is to grow and succeed. This is much easier said than done since it is rare that anyone should share the researcher's knowledge and experience of the new technology. In cases where the new technology is aimed at existing markets, the researcher entrepreneur needs to be able to "infect" others with the same vision and excitement. The sticking point is that while this may be possible with workers in the enterprise, it is much more difficult to convince prospective users and customers. This requires special persuasion and balancing skills and above all a capability for *assessing* the market.

The single word that may describe an entrepreneur best of all is *astute*. The online Oxford Dictionary defines an astute person as "having the ability to accurately assess situations or people and turn this to one's advantage". I think this is the precise characteristic that distinguishes a successful researcher entrepreneur. Learning to evaluate and assess situations, people, facts, and events and turn them to one's advantage is indeed the hallmark of all successful entrepreneurs. It takes a lot of time – and many attempts, some failed – to reach this level of experience, but it can be done.

The question, then, becomes the following: can a researcher learn to take management decisions quickly when the facts are only half-known or even unknown and when, crucially, business advisers cannot agree on which direction to follow? This is of course a case of risk management, and we'll come across many other such risks as well as appropriate management strategies later in this book.

These are not lessons that one can learn as such, but skills that one acquires with time and experience. A degree in effective management may help, but only a little. And a degree in higher level management (such as an MBA) is mainly useful regarding market research and some aspects of marketing, at least until the company (hopefully) grows. The rest is down to acquiring vital and diverse experiences in real time as you navigate setbacks and pitfalls, design and refine your vision, and make on-the-spot decisions in the fast-changing world of enterprise.

Experience proves particularly useful in the opportunities it offers for learning from one's failures. More often than not, one acquires many critical entrepreneurship skills from past attempts (sometimes failed, sometimes abandoned) at running an enterprise, especially attempts at entrepreneurial technology transfer. In a later chapter, we will consider the tremendous usefulness of intermediate failures in more detail, especially with regard to how they can pave the way towards success by serving as illuminating trial runs for your enterprise.

In Summary

In research we usually have ample time to decide on an important question, e.g. on the next steps in a research project, and we only take them after we gather all the information we need. When running a start-up, this luxury is, more often than not, simply not available. The life of a start-up entrepreneur – especially one operating in a competitive sector – can be summed simply as "decisions". Decisions on production, on marketing, on the new design or the alternative material, on staffing, on funding, on the new partner, etc. need to be continuously made even when information is incomplete.

An Invention Is not an Innovation 5

Consider for a moment how many patents are filed every year – nowadays, in their tens of thousands worldwide. And now consider how many innovations based on these patents actually reach the market or industry. The sad truth is that this number is very small indeed – perhaps a few dozen, maximum a few hundred, of which only a handful actually become market successes.

As I wrote in the TT Guide, an Invention is not necessarily an Innovation – all technology transfer attempts must proceed from this understanding. Only when the invention (i.e. your technology at TRL 4 and with protected status) has been fully developed via all the pilot and field tests does it acquire sufficient *value* – in direct relation to the need or demand for it – to become an innovation (at TRL 6 or 7) and the possible subject of a start-up company which would then bring it to TRL 8 and then 9. Figure 1.1 and Table 23.1 in the TT Guide illustrate this very well by introducing the three Critical Milestones (CM). While reaching the first CM ("Proof of Concept") only gives assurance that the concept is valid and *may* lead to some actual application if developed further, reaching the second CM means that the *technical feasibility* of the new idea is now proven for the chosen application. It is at this time that the industrial feasibility needs to be tested via pilot and industrial tests and this can be done either in the lab or in a start-up which should lead to the third CM (TRL8), which means that the *techno-economic viability* of the new technology is now assured and commercialisation can proceed.

There is another very important reason for developing your technology until at least TRL 6 before attempting to continue via a start-up: it is generally much more costly to do the industrial tests after setting up a start-up company, especially if you have to purchase instruments and lab facilities. Considering others' but also my own experiences, pilot-level RD in a well-run research laboratory is generally much cheaper and more effective to carry out than in a small company, unless the start-up is benefitting from direct and close contact with a laboratory.

An important lesson to draw from this, then, is the following: don't rush to set up a start-up only on the basis of an invention – even if it is well protected and appears very promising. Make sure it has proved its worth by testing it in the laboratory against all possible competing solutions under a range of conditions and in as many of its potential applications as possible to bring it as close as possible to the level of an innovative product or process. Otherwise, the business risk is too high.

It is the innovation that should be the subject of the start-up company, not the invention. In fact, you'd be very hard-pressed to get any competitive funding if your business plan is only based on an idea or an invention and has not been through pilot and field testing conclusively enough to offer more than just a good promise. To evaluators, the appeal and promise of your invention that are so obvious to you will only be interpreted as wishful thinking if you cannot show conclusively that you can offer a value-adding innovation which is at the right time and place rather than simply an invention, however promising it is. And don't forget that the value of the innovation is always judged in relation to the market and is not inherent in the technology.

To illustrate this point, remember the time when Google announced that its Google Glass™ device would stop being sold and the business unit restructured. [1] Although the announcement was cloaked in "we will push ahead" kind of talk, it was obvious that the device was not doing well at all in the market. As the Wall Street Journal remarked, "... sales were small amid complaints about privacy, technical shortcomings and a lack of obvious uses", not to mention that the device is banned in most normal places of gathering such as bars, cinemas, cafés, banks, casinos, hospitals, and so on. In other words, a very promising, technically highly developed invention that must have cost billions to develop never became a valuable innovation for the company mostly because of market reasons. It was seen as unworkable and it thus offered no clear *value* in relation to the market and consumer expectations; it was a promising invention but it never became an *innovation*. Even recent, more advanced versions never caught on.

An earlier example is that of the Segway™, the self-balancing personal transporter. After development that cost many millions, it only sold a few tens of thousands of units despite being available for more than 10 years. [2] The reason again was social. While the technology itself was brilliant, many people felt uncomfortable being seen on one, something that many successful entrepreneurs had warned. It certainly didn't help that the founder of the company was unfortunately himself killed when he steered his Segway off a cliff in 2010. The lesson is clear: no matter how brilliant an invention, its transformation into a successful innovative product is by no means guaranteed or automatic. No technology is valuable in and of itself. The *perception* of the market and the consumers is paramount.

Of course, as always, there are exceptions. I emphasised above that you should avoid going it alone via a start-up if your technology is still at an early TRL. If your

---

[1] Alistair Barr, 15 January 2015, "Google Glass Gets a New Direction: Tech Giant Stops Sales of First Generation Gadget and Restructures Unit", *The Wall Street Journal*. URL: http://www.wsj.com/articles/google-makes-changes-to-its-glass-project-1421343901.

[2] Jordan Golson, 16 January 2015, "Well, That Didn't Work: The Segway Is a Technological Marvel. Too Bad It Doesn't Make Any Sense", *Wired*. URL: http://www.wired.com/2015/01/well-didnt-work-segway-technological-marvel-bad-doesnt-make-sense/.

technology, however, is of a type that does not have any competitors and there is very clear and urgent need or demand for it, then the pilot tests and corresponding acceptance by the industry or the market may be shortened sufficiently to warrant the cost and risk of founding and supporting a start-up at an early stage. Some examples that fall into this category where a start-up at earlier TRLs has some chance of success include (but are not limited to) urgently required medicines (such as the recent Covid19 pandemic), technologies for environmental protection and remediation (where the environment has been damaged to such an extent that urgent measures are needed), and technologies needed to replace materials that have suddenly been found to be dangerous.

A number of examples of innovations developed via start-ups can help to clarify this. The 2015 Ebola epidemic in West Africa reached horrendous proportions before it was brought under control, and the only promising medicine at the time – produced by a start-up in Canada – was rushed through clinical trials in the hope of finding a successful solution. As a result, a promising medicine was developed within 1 year rather than the 10 years it usually takes for a medicine to be developed, a truly startling result. Vaccines are also being fast-tracked at the same time, at least one of them via a start-up company, and these look very promising too. The extremely fast development of mRNA vaccines for Covid19 (even if one takes into account the years of previous developments) is another successful example of extremely fast development that saved many thousands of lives and allowed us to return to normality.

A second example comes from the food sector. In the early 2000s, dioxin was detected on the surface of poultry sold in Europe and caused a serious food scare. The amount detected was in quantities which had recently been shown to be dangerous (though lower than the guidelines in force at the time), findings which subsequently led to a proposal to restrict the acceptable levels of dioxin in food by a factor of about 100. The problem was the absence at the time of any standard technique for measuring such low levels (parts per trillion, ppt) routinely, as would be required by industry. A European Commission-funded project was initiated based on a technology which developed the technique very rapidly and commercialised it – starting from a TRL of 3 – via a start-up in less than 3 years. The start-up route was deemed necessary to allow for faster development and since there was not enough time to negotiate with an existing manufacturer. As far as I know, it is still the only technique that can measure dioxin at levels of ppt.

A final example of setting up a start-up to commercialise a technology which is still at an early TRL is from the shoe industry. About 15 years ago, new, very strict regulations were enacted in Europe restricting the use of aromatic hydrocarbon-based glues. This led to a scramble to develop water-based glues (a number of relevant projects were funded by the EC, all starting at about TRL 3), and at least one was successfully commercialised by a start-up company after early development and patenting to TRL 5. A point of interest here is that few – if any – such glues existed before whereas now nearly all shoes sold in Europe are made using aqueous glues.

Another reason for taking the risk of setting up a start-up company at an early stage is if your technology is not (or cannot be) protected easily. The activities of a small company are much easier to protect than those of a research laboratory (with students, etc.), and the start-up route allows you the freedom of confidential development under very controlled conditions. I have personally set up a start-up company in the ceramics and minerals sectors for a processing technology which was at TRL 4 at the time and which could not be fully protected, even under a European patent. Working on my own allowed me the freedom of confidential pilot and industrial development even though it cost more in the long run.

These are of course the exceptions that prove the rule. Successfully commercialised technologies that were rushed through the stages are rare and nearly always the result of a major external push (financial, social, etc.) due to an urgent and unforeseen need. Most times, commercialisation success comes though systematic conversion of an invention to an innovation without skipping or rushing though any stages. This holds true whether the commercialisation was effected via a start-up or any other route.

In Summary

An invention does not a valuable innovation make without hard work. It is very rare for an early-stage technology – i.e. at the invention stage – to be commercialised successfully. In the vast majority of cases, all inventions – i.e. ideas whose concept have been proof-tested and developed as inventions – need to be further converted to innovative products or services by a transformation process. It's well neigh impossible to succeed in the market without effective protection, without validated technical feasibility for the particular application, without careful field testing and scaling up and especially without techno-economic viability validation.

6

Opportunities Are Everywhere… and if There Aren't, Create Them!

The decision to set up a start-up company by a researcher or an inventor is generally based on a new and well-developed technology which promises to successfully address a potential industrial or market need or demand. But this decision does not only have to be reactionary, that is, responding to an *existing* need. An inspiration for a start-up can arise even when there is no need currently in evidence. The researcher entrepreneur can *create* or *foresee* advantageous business opportunities where opportunities do not at present exist by leveraging special situations and events. Various instabilities or imbalances in the market or society may indicate where future technological need may develop. The shrewd researcher entrepreneur will constantly be on the lookout and recognise such conditions as fertile ground for the future development of needs or demands and therefore prepare or search for new technologies accordingly. It is this capability for coupling *current* or *potential* needs with technologies that makes a successful entrepreneur.

In enterprise, the researcher entrepreneur may do one of two things in response to a perceived or identified business opportunity. The first refers to the need or demand for which a technology is not yet available, in which case an astute researcher entrepreneur may embark on a project to develop it further and, in parallel, to create a need for it. The second route involves adapting an existing technology or using it differently to fit the identified market need or demand.

Both of the above cases describe the identification of the business *opportunity*. In the former, it is the opportunity offered by the technology's capabilities and promise; in the latter, it is the opportunity offered by a market need which points the way to a successful business. In both cases, the raison d'être of a start-up is to exploit the promise and maximise the benefit from such opportunities.

Industrial companies are always an excellent source of technological business opportunities for innovative solutions and products – as long as one can find out their specific technological needs, which is often very difficult. A manufacturer is always loath to let their competitors (or the market) know that they are having technical difficulties or that their existing operations are less than optimum and therefore, in an effort to improve their operations, could be interested in finding new processes or devices or materials to replace their existing ones. This is a well-recognised major obstacle to technology transfer from the lab for technologies which have been developed without a specific target in mind, the so-called "technology push" approach.

But even if such an industrial need is identified, it is usually extremely difficult to connect with the decision-makers in large companies who would take the decision to test new technologies in order to improve their operations. To bridge this gap, over the past 20 years or so technology brokers (also called "innovation brokers") have been posting many such open innovation calls to solve various generic or specific industrial needs. Two examples of larger brokers are Innocentive™ (www.innocentive.com, now called wazoku.com) and NineSigma™ (www.ninesigma.com), but a number of smaller ones specialised in niche markets are also very active.

Even if one cannot find specific industrial problems to solve, business opportunities are everywhere. In fact, any kind of instability, breakthrough, or imbalance may give rise to technological business opportunities. In the TT Guide, I discussed at length the many everyday sources of ideas for technologies that have led to a plethora of products over the past years. I also discussed the importance of identifying a need even before it becomes apparent, so that you can have the time to develop new solutions and direct them towards addressing the emerging need.

An excellent case in point is the meteoric rise in social networking provided by tech start-ups such as Facebook™, Twitter™, LinkedIn™, TikTok™, etc. Although the need for a more convenient, fast, easy-access, and multi-platform communication among the increasingly internationalised and tech-savvy millennial generation had become apparent for years, especially after Internet access and personal computing had become widely available, it was the development of social networking websites that offered the viable solution. These offered both better communication *and* a community where people can interact and find others with similar interests. As a business opportunity, the need and demand was already identified and pending, but the difficulty was in identifying it, analysing it, and then offering this added value that succeeded where other solutions had failed. In fact, other approaches had already failed before these ones managed to excite the public and succeed in getting huge followings. For example, before Facebook™, there was MySpace™ which folded after a brief period, perhaps because it did not offer just the right type of services, or because it was too early to take advantage of the developing social networking avalanche.

All types of instabilities and imbalances, whether negative or positive, can give rise to successful technological enterprises, as indicated in Fig. 6.1. While the Internet – probably the single most important technological overhaul since the industrial revolution in the nineteenth century – brought about a revolution in communications, information availability, knowledge production and dissemination, and entertainment, it also gave rise to many misuses and abuses. Both of these directions – constructive and destructive – are types of instability that have been recognised as such and that have been the source of countless technological developments and associated enterprises.

Fig. 6.1 Breakthroughs, instabilities, or imbalances are all fertile grounds for new technological enterprises

Currently, serious problems of online abuse in the form of so-called trolling (malicious anonymous attacks on a mass scale) on numerous sites with commenting and messaging features (such as Twitter™ and Facebook™) have arisen which have proved particularly difficult to deal with. Nevertheless, the application of specialist stochastic algorithms is already providing viable solutions to such problems. The online world is replete with examples illustrating the legal and cultural gaps regarding its proper regulation and the ways in which digital spaces are utilised, and the demand for new technologies (e.g. encryption solutions, e-readers, new types of online sharing and connecting communities) is strong, which in itself presents excellent opportunities for an astute entrepreneur.

Numerous ingenious apps have been written for and are used on smartphones. Most of these have arisen not through direct identification of a need which required a solution, but as an added capability in our everyday lives. Such enhancements may not offer solutions to serious obstacles or needs, but are nevertheless welcomed by users for their novelty, fascination, and/or use value. They range from microscope attachments to radiation scanners to key finders to child monitors, and they are all examples of successful (to varying degrees) technological entrepreneurship.

Artificial intelligence (AI) is also developing very fast, mainly as a means to derive benefit from huge databases that have been built up with various data, personal or otherwise. But AI has now developed into many different directions, all based on reinforcement-based "machine learning" algorithms. On the one hand, AI programs offer very good pattern recognition capabilities (e.g. for symptom-based or optical medical diagnosis, for word-pattern analyses and for feature or face recognition, etc.), and on the other hand, they generate quick synopses, analyses, and text on the basis of prompts, based on previously acquired and "digested" text from huge databases (e.g. from online encyclopaedias). This type of generative AI is often misleading as there seems very little control on how real text is digested and used to generate analyses with the result that in many instances the results are erroneous or just plain fake. In addition, a huge problem is now recognised that many, if not all, of these programmes have actually used and digested copyrighted and proprietary online materials (texts, graphics or photos) without permission. An interesting legal tussle is now brewing and it'll be interesting to see how it'll turn out. In addition, the instabilities can also be initiated by policy design or politics. New visions (e.g. space exploration, environmental protection), political decisions, shifting alliances, boycotts, and embargoes all give rise to significant opportunities for technological entrepreneurship. Although such opportunities may not be very long-lived, they nevertheless can play a major role in the economic development of whole countries. The international boycott of apartheid-era South Africa (late 1980s) is an interesting case in point. Because of the boycott, the government at the time funded and tried to develop self-sufficiency in all areas affected by the boycott, especially technological areas including manufacturing and chemicals. In many areas, they succeeded. The result was a major entrepreneurship drive, led by researchers and inventors, which resulted in an increase in GNP for the first few years. Naturally, such a push was not sustainable as most of the enterprises formed (ironically) did not have access to sufficient markets for their products. Many therefore failed after a few years even with huge state support, and it was mainly this severe economic imbalance (in addition to activists' and liberation struggles) which eventually precipitated the fall of apartheid by the early 1990s.

Interestingly, a similar situation is developed in Europe about 10 years ago due to the (apparently political) decision of China to restrict exports of many critical raw materials used in electronics, including rare earth metals. Over the last decades, mining of many metals has all but ceased in Europe, in large part because of the much lower production costs (and more lax environmental safeguards) in China. However, the export restrictions announced about 10 years ago by China quickly led to an upsurge in production in Europe and re-classification of many such materials as "strategic" and therefore subsidisable. More interestingly, this has led to strong research efforts to develop substitutes for these critical materials for the same applications. The range of such "critical materials" is very large indeed: all rare earths (used in magnets and electronics), most of the platinum group metals (catalysts, etc.), many of the transition metals (magnets, electronics, specialist structural, chemical applications, etc.), refractory metals and ceramics (high temperature use), and many others. The fact that in nearly all cases straightforward substitution by other (non-critical) materials is not actually all that simple has resulted in a large worldwide effort for innovative solutions to this challenge.

All the above are good examples of opportunities brought about by both externally led and internally driven decisions which became fertile grounds for new businesses.

Of course, as mentioned previously, opportunities can also be created by the actions of researchers themselves, even in the absence of a specific market pull. I am referring to many successful technologies (and enterprises) that did not initially directly address a need or demand, but were nevertheless originated by researchers who, as astute entrepreneurs, managed to create the demand by clever marketing and by encouraging users themselves to find ways to utilise them. They are now at the heart of successful enterprises, many offered under larger platforms. Examples are online games, quizzes, and tests, many aspects of social networking, targeted specialist advertising, AI text and analyses preparation, and others.

Interesting opportunities are also sometimes found in the field of standardisation and testing. Over the years, many national and international standard organisations under the banners of BS (British), DIN (German), ASTM (USA), ISO (International), EN (European Union), etc. have tried to standardise testing of materials and systems to ensure reliable comparison of results between countries and have issued a huge number of standard procedures, many of which can be interpreted and applied in various ways. This freedom of interpretation, therefore, may allow an inventor to find a new method for applying such a procedure for a specific application.

The recognition of a good opportunity for an innovative technological application is the sign of a good researcher entrepreneur: one who sees his or her research results not only as a new piece of knowledge but also as a potential product or service ready to acquire flesh and blood in the future.

In Summary

Opportunities for technology commercialisation almost never appear out of the blue asking for someone to exploit them. A researcher needs to look carefully in their "box of inventions" and then consider which of them could interest the industry or the market at that moment in time. On the other hand, instabilities, imbalances, and breakthroughs in the market may very well present opportunities which a researcher could exploit by developing specific solutions to address them.

Can You Manage as well as You Research?

Not everyone is cut out to be an entrepreneur who thrives under adversity. And the everyday world of research is as far removed from the world of business as it gets.

Most researchers and inventors spend much of their careers in a laboratory, doing what they know best: thinking up new ideas and inventions and working on them till they prove the concept and produce a working laboratory prototype. They work diligently and try to understand and analyse their subject as deeply as possible. They are driven by *curiosity*, by the need to understand their environment and by the satisfaction of discovery. If their discovery or invention has an obvious application, so much the better, but this is generally not the main motivation.

A discovery or an invention needs to be very carefully tested and analysed, especially in comparison to what is already known. As a result, a researcher needs to be precise and accurate and to have persistence and perseverance. Risks are generally not taken and any unknowns are carefully clarified before moving on. Researchers simply cannot afford to be gung-ho about their work! Understanding human psychology is rarely a necessity for a technological researcher. Neither is a deep understanding of human responses to a technological offering, as marketing requires.

In contrast to a researcher, however, an entrepreneur requires many, very diverse skills in order to be successful. Deep understanding of the technology that forms the core of their business is not necessary, but understanding the capabilities and competitiveness of the particular technology vis-à-vis the competition is crucial as well as the extent of its feasibility for satisfying a need or demand, which is often the deciding factor. Furthermore, the cost-benefit (i.e. the viability) offered for a particular application is a strong measure of its competitiveness in a market where other solutions already exist. Other management skills, which a researcher rarely possesses or is experienced in, are also necessary. Negotiating skills are a must both with one's personnel and with other business entities. Understanding of market trends and the capability of forecasting and foresighting future market positions and trends are also crucial for successful entrepreneurship. Above all else, however, an entrepreneur understands and manages entrepreneurial risk.

I mentioned risk management previously as well: this is often the chief trait that many identify as the crucial point of differentiation between the two worlds. But risk management does not mean a headlong rush into taking risky decisions and carrying out risky investments, and it should certainly not be perceived as a stand-in for damage control! Risk management refers to the critical capability of judging the level of risk vis-à-vis the outcome, whether this is beneficial or problematic. It is the ability that good entrepreneurs possess of making *rapidly* a carefully *weighed guesstimate* of the possibility of a risky scenario going one way or another and preparing for both outcomes. Whereas a researcher rarely takes risks (if he or she can help it), an entrepreneur often takes risks where he or she judges that they have a good chance of yielding good returns.

Regarding risk, it is important to point out the misunderstanding on the part of many researchers of the level of technological development needed by the industry of any technology in order to be accepted for industrial use. Whereas in the lab our aim is to fully understand all facets of a technology, often going deeper and deeper into the science, industry is mainly interested in "fit for purpose" level of development and no further. It is a case of balancing the cost of RD development against expected returns. This is another aspect where an experienced entrepreneur would know where to draw the line. A similar situation arises when a certain level of flexibility and compromise is necessary in response to what is needed by the market in comparison to what it is possible to achieve within the time available and with the level of investment at one's disposal in a start-up. The market will not wait forever and competing technologies are often at one's heels.

It seems therefore that there exists a dichotomy in some of the critical and distinguishing traits that characterise a good researcher and a good entrepreneur, respectively. Whereas there is a great deal of crossover between the skill sets of the researcher and the entrepreneur and they both share similar positive traits/strengths, as we saw in the first chapter, it is their respective approaches to their technology and its applicability vis-à-vis the market that set them apart. This difference in approach and outlook is a major obstacle in convincing a researcher to transfer their technology via a start-up company. This is why it is rare to find a researcher who is also a good entrepreneur.

So what is the solution? A clear answer presents itself: if you are a researcher who does not have entrepreneurial experience, then you should seriously consider going into partnership with an experienced professional manager who will run your company with you. There really is no better alternative.

A collaborative venture of this sort – in which the skills of the researcher and the experienced manager are pooled to make for a much more convincing research-business duo – may sound like an obvious decision to take. However, many researchers and academics who have developed a technology with excellent prospects take the entrepreneurial plunge with scant regard for their own entrepreneurial capabilities in the apparent belief that one can simply learn the ropes as one goes along – all too often with sadly predictable results. Sometimes this can appear to be vanity combined with a misguided attraction to the power of running one's own company which propels them to set up a start-up without a full understanding of the crucial advantages (and risk reduction) that a collaboration or cooperation with a business-savvy partner brings.

Some time ago, I was asked to support a struggling spin-off that had found itself in danger of bankruptcy even though its core technology was clearly competitive in its field. The problem turned out to be a classical case of a researcher not willing to recognise that he lacked the necessary skills (and time) to manage his company properly. As a result, his clearly competitive technology was left by the wayside when the main potential customer made its choice among the new technologies available (in this case a new production process). A crucial mistake that this owner-researcher made was this: as a consummate researcher, he believed that his technology needed an ever greater level of fine-tuning and micromanaged the technological development well beyond what was necessary for the customer's needs. His overemphasis on further development – beyond the "fit-for-purpose" benchmark – resulted in him being scared to take the risk to expose the new technology to the market. For this researcher, the technology would never be "good" enough to be accepted by the market. The result at the end of the day was predictable. A rival technology won the contract and proceeded to develop further within the customer's operations, as a technology partner. Unfortunately, the spin-off company (based in the Netherlands) with the otherwise very promising and competitive technology was still struggling to get off the ground last time I heard and never achieved sufficient market penetration.

Another example I recall is the case of a small spin-off from a university which had developed a cheaper alternative to a recycling process for a range of alloys. However, the researcher failed to check that the price of the metals that they could recycle suddenly rose so high that their technology could have entered the market successfully at an earlier stage (thereby spending much less on development) instead of waiting until it had reached the level of development aimed for at the start. By the time the researcher was satisfied with the high level of extraction of their new technology, the market had already accepted a rival, cheaper recycling technology, even though it was less efficient. Rapidly shifting market developments passed this researcher by – mainly because they were not watching the outside developments carefully –and the opportunity was lost.

Not all such cases finish negatively. An academic I worked with some years ago decided to try his hand at entrepreneurship to bring a new technology he had developed to industry (a new way of removing polluting organic molecules from water with extremely high selectivity and sensitivity). He discovered within a few months that entrepreneurship is a full-time job and found that he couldn't handle it in parallel with his research and teaching. He has since gone into partnership with a young post-doc who has a background in both Chemistry and Economics who has worked very hard in managing the company and getting the industrial testing completed. Her commitment and dual expertise combined with his technological acumen has meant that they developed their first commercial product (a type of membrane filter) very quickly and are now fairly successful. This was indeed a win-win situation since they both got the work satisfaction they wanted with a clear long-term (potential) benefit.

Unfortunately, this is not as frequent as one would wish. Many other examples exist of researchers trying to go alone with their own start-ups but making several unfortunate management mistakes that recur time and time again in such cases of attempted technology transfer. I hope the cases presented above have helped to illuminate some of these, such as mismanaging funds, not being able to "read the market" correctly, and even misunderstanding the needs of the market.

Most researchers may be excellent at developing their technologies in the lab, but the market requires a very different approach and mindset. A good researcher is not always the best manager for his or her own start-up company, and this is an important lesson one has to identify early on before moving from the lab world to the business world.

In Summary

An entrepreneur needs a more diverse set of management skills than a researcher. Most researchers may be excellent at developing their technologies in the lab, but the market requires a very different approach and mindset. Because most – if not all – responsibility for the company rests on their shoulders, start-up entrepreneurs need to be good at overseeing and managing people, design, production, marketing, sales, etc.

Strong Foundations

8

Just as "a journey of a thousand miles begins with a single step" [1], so an enterprise is founded on specific preparatory steps that a researcher must take and prerequisites that must be fulfilled before he or she attempts the transition. The initial stages should be carried out while the researcher is still in his or her laboratory, while the latter deal with the setting up of the enterprise as such. As Fig. 8.1 illustrates, there are many aspects that constitute foundation pillars of the new enterprise, ranging from technological quality to funding and engineering. Let's consider them in sequence to see how they naturally lead into and support one another.

The most important foundation pillar is the scientific and technological quality of the technology. It goes without saying that if the technology is not developed to the highest possible quality and completeness for the application it is aimed at (i.e. fit for purpose, not more), it will not find it easy to enter the market. Even though time is very often of the essence in successful market entry, rushing through the development of the technology is never a good idea. Trying to complete too quickly the final stages of technological development while managing a company is tantamount to driving a car while the mechanic is still trying to repair it. A fudged technology is likely to ensue that cannot hope to gain market entry.

Related to the importance of ensuring high quality for the technology is its applicability. The importance of coupling the technology to one or more applications as early as possible is paramount and critical for its later adoption; yet its potential applicability is very often not considered seriously by the researchers themselves in the early stages of its development. Unless it is a generic technology, such as a new material or phenomenon, its development must always be carried out in tandem with its targeted application or applications.

Once the technology is fully developed in the lab – already targeted for a particular market entry – it is its competitiveness that counts. This includes effective

---

[1] Lao Tzu (Sixth Century BCE Chinese philosopher, founder of Taoism), quoted at URL: http://www.quotationspage.com/quote/24004.html

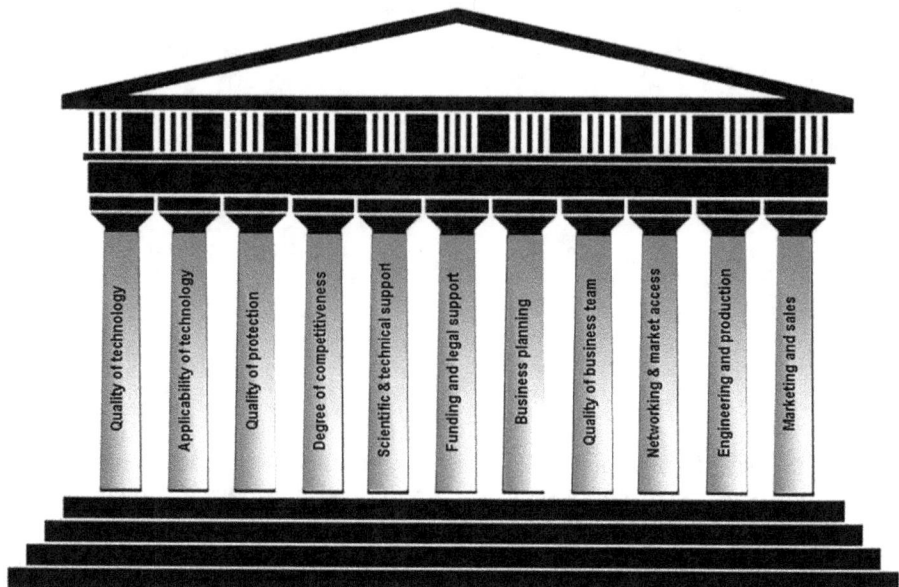

Fig. 8.1 The quality and completeness of the foundation pillars are critical for the success of the enterprise

protection, high technical competitiveness, and high market viability, i.e. a very high benefit-to-cost ratio. Furthermore, more often than not, it is the capability of maintaining the competitive edge over time that will determine the success of the whole enterprise. This is why the quality and long-term efficacy of the protection strategy are so crucial and must be prepared well before any steps are taken to set up a company.

Effective protection of a technology ensures fair returns for your efforts in developing it. The first step in developing a strong protection strategy is to ensure that the technology you have developed is in the right shape to form the bedrock of a new enterprise. This means that the technology must be developed at least to TRL 4 (preferably TRL 5) and its technical feasibility proven under conditions as close as possible to the market or industry conditions in which it will be further developed in the next steps. Once that is ensured, you can decide on the optimum protection strategy. This is discussed in more detail in the TT Guide, but essentially it can either entail formal protection (i.e. a patenting strategy), informal protection (i.e. confidentiality), or a hybrid strategy where you patent the generic aspects and keep the key aspects confidential. Beyond these, there are other, more nuanced routes to successful protection which depend on aspects such as the degree of novelty of the technology and the extent to which it can be *recognised* or *identified* as novel, the extent to which it can be reverse-engineered, the capability of obstructing and/or detecting counterfeits, the degree of exposure, if it is embedded in an integrated system, the degree of advancement over its competitors, etc. An effective protection strategy is a major pillar of a successful enterprise and will be discussed further later on in this book.

The achievement of a complete and competitive technology is of course the result of scientific and technological research excellence. This excellence is not only necessary during the development phases, but also, very importantly, during the industrial development, product design, and eventually during engineering and production as well. In all of these stages, the highest level of scientific and technological support is critical since it is to be expected that many changes and adaptations of the technology will be necessary before it can be rolled out onto the market.

All of the above pillars comprise the technological part of the Business Plan for your prospective enterprise. Your *business plan* is where your whole idea for the enterprise comes together in one complete document with detailed descriptions of all the pillars and your suggested approach to addressing them. Your business plan will also include many other pillars, detailing funding, legal status, contracts, management, skills and personnel, engineering and production, marketing and sales, and so on and so forth. It is a major document that shows, in full detail, how you intend to make your technology the object of a successful technology transfer process via a new start-up company.

We have already mentioned crucial foundation pillars relating to the technological dimension of your prospective enterprise. Other important pillars in the business dimension include the following (not an exhaustive list). Funding has to be secured not only for the initial setting-up expenses but also for any unforeseen costs, until you start receiving income. The legal status of the company must be decided so that the company is not only secure but *seen* as secure by potential supporters and funding bodies. Good, skilled, and trustworthy personnel have to be found to help you run the company. Right from the outset, design and engineering will play a major role since the industrial development of the technology needs to be carried out hand in hand with the production strategy. Finally, and of equal importance, marketing strategy will have to be decided and sales routes secured. We'll discuss many of these important enterprise-related aspects in more detail later.

All of the foundation pillars mentioned here are interlinked and co-dependent. They are also all dependent on one of the most important pillars of all: *networking*. Networking involves forging supporting connections and establishing trust, in research as well as in business. Above and beyond any other consideration, it is networking that can make the difference between grinding to a halt or finding a solution to the many serious obstacles that are almost certainly going to appear on the entrepreneurial road to success. Since no modern enterprise can be built based entirely on the shoulders of one individual alone, no matter how talented, plucky, persevering, or hard-working that individual may be, he or she needs to establish strong and effective networks in all aspects of his or her company as early as possible. Networking is a process of mutual trust and mutual support and as such is an indispensable element in any researcher entrepreneur's toolkit.

In fact, many of the other pillars will benefit from – if not crucially depend on – strong and effective networks. For example, during the industrial testing or engineering development, it may be an expert collaborator from a previous project that you may have to call upon to help. And your good standing and excellent reputation, as attested by your network, will help you in times when funding will be needed for the next steps. Most importantly, it will be your network of collaborators that you'll turn to for industrial support to enter a new market and secure the first critical installations or demonstrations.

Strong foundations for a new enterprise are like the actual foundations of a building: build them so that they are secure and long-lasting and you will have a head start on your road to entrepreneurial success.

In Summary

A start-up (or spin-off) enterprise is founded on specific preparatory steps that a researcher must take and prerequisites that must be fulfilled before they attempt the transition. The initial stages should be carried out while the researcher is still in his or her laboratory, while the latter deal with the setting up of the enterprise as such. By building strong foundations so that they are secure and long-lasting, you will have a head start on your road to entrepreneurial success.

Aim for Perfection 9

You may have heard the advice offered by many: that in order to succeed in entrepreneurship, reaching the market fast takes precedence over perfecting your technology. It most certainly should not. While timing is highly important, it is even more central that one presents a technological solution that addresses the identified need and does so better than any other. And all within the time constraints dictated by the market. A very tall order but by no means impossible to attain.

Your technology, no matter what it is, will be subjected to very close scrutiny, both in terms of what it can do toward satisfying the identified need and vis-à-vis any competing technologies. This level of scrutiny means that you cannot afford to offer a less than perfect product! You only have one chance to impress the market and you need to put all you have into it. You may be forced to take risks in other areas (market timing, price, etc.), but you should not take any risks relating to quality or effectiveness.

The need for the highest possible quality and effectiveness notwithstanding every technology has its performance limits. It is with these limits in mind that you will aim to establish technological perfection. What you need to do is to identify those limits and push against them to reach the highest possible level of technological perfection. Such limits may be absolute, perhaps dictated by the laws of physics, so perfection means to get as close as possible to these theoretical limits, or they could be relative limits as dictated by comparison with other, competitive technologies in the market or under preparation. A successful technology may thus be the result of beating another technology in performance, design, functionality, etc.

Perfection *per se* has many facets. It may refer to the quality of manufacture, functionality (crucial, especially with respect to the competition), design, cost-benefit, user-friendliness, compatibility, etc. All of these parameters are important, and they should all be optimised as much as possible, especially if they are essential for the use that the technology will be put to. Each of these parameters is at a different criticality level depending on the type of technology you are developing. For example, a consumer product must not only be functional and user-friendly, but it must be seen to be so, i.e. the design is also very important and must make the technology's functionality obvious at a glance. At the other end of the spectrum, an industrial technology which will be incorporated in some system should be "perfect" only as far as functionality, performance, and quality of materials are concerned. Outward design plays a smaller role here and therefore need only be "perfected" as far as its actual fitness is at stake. It is a balancing game that requires prioritising different areas of energy and time expenditure appropriately so that fitness for purpose is achieved.

The field of computer gaming provides plenty of examples to illustrate this last point. In the early days of computing, games were designed and built by semi-amateurs and as a result were "rough and ready". Computer monitors were monochrome and capabilities limited. As computing power increased and coloured monitors became ubiquitous, game design became more and more important. A whole new ball-park started opening up where the original games looked out of place and gradually lost followers. Those games that managed to revamp themselves and display some flair (i.e. design) succeeded, even though functionality was (in those early stages) only marginally better. Nowadays, games are so advanced that very often I struggle to decide if I'm looking at a real-life video or a game!

Aiming for perfection is important in all aspects of a technology but at no time more so than when your technology is aiming to enter a market that is already dominated by other products. New smartphones, cars, computer games, and so on all have to be extremely well engineered and presented in order to gain any traction in the market. Industrial processes that aim to replace existing processes need to display very high added value (i.e. perfection in functionality and operation) in order to be considered as a potential replacement.

As always, aiming for perfection should be balanced against industry or market needs. There is no sense in spending huge efforts and money for a marginal improvement in functionality which is not essential for market or industry acceptance. In any case, as we mentioned above and shall discuss in more detail later, perfection is often not an absolute quantity but instead entails "striking the right balance" between efforts (i.e. investment) and added value or benefit.

Aiming for perfection is also of huge importance in its own right since, as a process, it is a very important learning curve. In any case, even if you don't reach perfection, you'll learn a huge amount trying. After every failed attempt to reach perfection, the knowledge gained will be invaluable and help you to correct mistakes and improve your chances. We'll look more closely at the benefits that failed attempts offer in Chap. 27, where we will encounter the (unofficial) motto of the young entrepreneurs in California's Silicon Valley: "Fail often, fail fast".

Additionally, perfection should be striven toward in all aspects of managing a company, not just in technological quality and capability. Successful entrepreneurship depends on the effectiveness of marketing, sales routes and methods, costing and pricing, branding, production methods, as well as management style and personnel satisfaction. All of these aspects of running a company can be thought of as parts of a puzzle. The whole picture can only be appreciated if all the pieces are in place. And the whole picture is only as perfect as the parts that constitute it.

9 Aim for Perfection

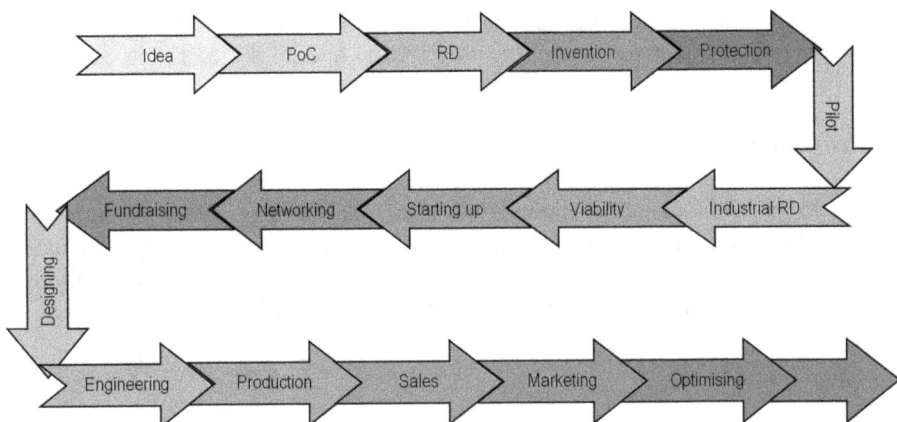

Fig. 9.1 All links in the development and commercialisation chain must be as strong as possible to ensure the integrity of the whole chain

An enterprise based on a new technology can be thought of as a chain with many links, each leading into and supporting the next. From the idea, to the proof of concept and the invention, all the way to the market innovation and market success, the chain is continuous and the quality of each link is crucial for the strength of the whole chain, as illustrated in Fig. 9.1 If any of these links is weak, it affects the integrity of the whole chain which loses most of its value. Aiming for perfection in all aspects of technological entrepreneurship ensures the maximum quality of each link and the chain as a whole.

Aiming for perfection is especially important at the three Critical Milestones identified and discussed in the TT Guide: the Proof of Concept, the Technical Feasibility test, and the Viability (cost-benefit) test. If any of these milestones are weak, then the whole chain from there onwards will be built on shaky ground. In addition to ensuring quality at these three Critical Milestones, all of the foundation pillars in Fig. 8.1 should be prepared and be the conjoined outcome of your drive for perfection.

Someone might very well interject here and declare, "perfection is impossible anyway—why bother?" Indeed, actual perfection is indeed impossible, but setting your sights at the highest possible level of quality and overall effectiveness will allow you to identify and address many more potential (and actual) obstacles, thereby preparing you for any eventualities in the future. Aiming for perfection will force you to consider (many) different routes and solutions as well as many useful "what if" scenario for the development of your enterprise. In so doing, once the time comes to actually set up your start-up, you will avoid the many false starts and pitfalls that line the path of every new entrepreneur.

Last but certainly not least, even if your enterprise does not reach the pinnacle you hoped for, aiming for perfection in all of its aspects will undoubtedly give you the satisfaction that you have tried your utmost.

As Thomas Watson Sr, the founder of IBM, once said, "It's better to aim for perfection and miss it, than to aim for imperfection and hit it" [1].

In Summary

Aiming for perfection is important in all aspects of a technology but at no time more so than when your innovation is aiming to enter a market that is already dominated by other products. As Thomas Watson of IBM famously said, "It's better to aim for perfection and miss it, than to aim for imperfection and hit it".

---

[1] Thomas J. Watson Sr. (Founder of IBM), quoted at URL: http://www.qotd.org/search/search.html?aid=6542

Strategise like a 5* General 10

The decision to set up an enterprise is only the beginning. Just like any campaign, in order for it to be successful, you have to have strong foundations. And strong foundations come from accurate strategic planning.

In all campaigns, complete, in-depth, and accurate planning is crucial. This includes planning of actions, activities, and strategies but also planning for the unforeseen. In many cases, planning for all eventualities – having a Plan B, and even a Plan C to hand – may prove to be more important later on than the business planning itself.

Business planning involves all of the aspects shown in Figs. 8.1 and 9.1 and, most importantly, it also involves crucial strategic decisions as follows:

- When is research and development enough so that I can start thinking about commercialisation?
- When and how to protect the technology?
- What are the pros and cons of protection *vs* open access?
- How much development is "just right"?
- How much and when to apply for funding? What type?
- At which stage in the economic cycle do I set up my company?
- At which stage in the investment cycle of my potential customers do I approach them?
- What are the characteristics of the ideal partner for investment or industrial development or market penetration?
- Which industry or market should I aim at first?
- Are there any other industries or markets I should aim at?
- What is the right pricing and marketing strategy for my product?
- Etc.

Clearly, every case should be treated on its own merits and characteristics. There are, however, some aspects common to all technology transfer processes that are worth mentioning briefly here. In the following chapters, a number of them will be addressed in more detail.

First of all, when should research be considered complete so that one should consider technology transfer and the setting up of a start-up company? The TT Guide describes this in more detail, but the rule of thumb is when the technology reaches TRL 4 or 5 and has successfully demonstrated Milestone 2. At this stage, the technical feasibility of the technology has been proven and little if any added value would result from further laboratory research. It is also the point at which protection would normally be considered.

Of course, reaching TRL 5 does not necessarily mean that your technology is now ready for commercialisation. Far from it, in fact. It still requires pilot testing and development, industrial testing, and most importantly viability testing to reach Milestone 3 where your technology would be considered techno-economically viable for the target application. Techno-economic viability refers to the fact that your technology's cost-effectiveness for the selected application must be high enough for customers to take notice.

In the TT Guide, I have made a point of the importance of the progression from Stage to Stage and from Milestone to Milestone via the planning and execution of specific activities. But it is not enough just to plan and carry out these activities from Milestone to Milestone. You have to work out clear strategies from the outset, strategies that will increase the probability of eventual success as an entrepreneur. Let's consider the most important of them briefly here while the following chapters will look at them in more detail.

Protection Strategy

In most cases, your protection strategy is pivotal for commercial success and should be selected with great care. As analysed in the TT Guide, there are essentially four main strategies that one can use for a new technology approaching TRL 4:

- Formal protection which entails patenting and other similar forms which offer a "legal monopoly" to the inventor for a number of years to produce and sell the technology by restricting others from using it.
- Informal protection which essentially entails keeping the technology secret and hoping that no one will think of it independently.
- A hybrid strategy in which some of the generic aspects of the technology (those that cannot be hidden) are patented and the key aspects (e.g. those processing conditions that optimise the technology) are kept secret.
- Open access to the technology keeping only some key aspects secret for niche uses. This is used when the technology is so completely novel that users need to become accustomed to it.

The strategy you choose will depend on a number of factors, most important of these being the level of difficulty involved in copying or reverse-engineering the technology. A few examples may help to illustrate the protection strategies outlined above. For instance, a new chemical should be patented only as far as its functionality is concerned, but the details of the process used to produce it must be kept secret. However, if the design of a technology can be easily copied, it should also be patented and monitored as far as possible. If on the other hand the technology is to be embedded, i.e. used as part of a device or system, it may pay to keep it secret. While specialised software is self-protected since the source code is generally not released, it may pay to have the "process" or method used to produce it protected formally. Finally, in the fourth route, a further level of hybrid strategy is used when a generic version of a technology is offered in open access, but any specialised versions are protected and offered commercially.

Funding Strategy

Funding strategy is one of the most difficult decisions involved in preparing a start-up company. Although certain advisers advocate that researcher entrepreneurs "get as much money as possible to be able to move as quickly as possible", I believe that the amount and type of funding should be very carefully weighed so as to avoid overshooting. The business plan should contain carefully argued financial needs vis-à-vis costs and projected income so that any funding decisions are taken based on this analysis. In general, the rule of thumb should be "accept only as much funding as you absolutely need until income commences". This may sound like common sense, but it is an error made frequently by start-ups where excess funding gets funnelled into unnecessary expenses and over-development which results in delays reaching the market and eventually achieving a break-even point. Avoiding unnecessary overdevelopment that takes your technology beyond the "fit-for-purpose" mark is another important strategic decision, since you should not expect to receive returns on superfluous investment. There is a time and a place to stop development, and these are all strategically determined. With regard to planning strategically for fitness for purpose, a tactic for market development may be pointed out here. By designing several different versions of a product, each based on a common basic technology but presenting different levels of capabilities (and functionality), one can cleverly produce "fit-for-purpose" products that cover the whole spectrum from the basic level to the highest. This strategy is often used in the automotive, mobile telephony, and computing industries, for example.

Nowadays, sources of funding for start-ups have multiplied and many types are available, ranging from the European Commission's "SME Instrument" and loan guarantees under the large Horizon funding programmes to various Venture Capital funds offering seed and pilot funding to bank or private loans. In addition, structural funds are earmarked for many developing states of the European Union; administered by national governments, many of these offer financial support to start-up companies. The common denominator of these different sources of funding is that at least 50% of the total costs must be covered by own funds or other private source(s). If a researcher relies on a loan to cover this part, such rules add a level of risk to the start-up company and to the researcher. The alternative is to find a private investor or a VC who will often take control of the company until expected profits are realised. More details are included in a later chapter.

Investment Cycle Timing Strategy

The condition of the economy and that of a potential adopting industry is an important parameter that should dictate the actual time when a start-up is set up. Market entry should be chosen when the market is at its most buoyant and mature (i.e. prepared for the technology) and the potential company is ready for re-investment in new technologies. By estimating the time that is required for the technology to reach the market, it is possible to reach a decision on optimum market entry. However, this is not essential if various products or versions of the technology are to be produced at various times.

In the case of technologies that are not aimed at direct market entry but for industrial use (e.g. to be used in production processes or embedded in production facilities), it may also be necessary to time the industrial development (i.e. the setting up of the start-up and the industrial RD) to coincide with the investment decisions of customers.

Partnership and Networking Strategies

To have a fighting chance, a start-up will need support from strong partners in all areas, and decisions about whom to collaborate with are serious strategic decisions in their own right. An investment partner must be able to understand the technology, the market, and the industry so that he or she will not have unreasonable expectations of the start-up's chances and prospects. On the other hand, an industrial development partner needs to understand the needs of the industry or market and also the capabilities of other competitive products or solutions. Finally, the market penetration partner must know the various markets and industries for the technology and understand their needs and demands in conjunction with their expectations and limits to be able to develop a good market penetration strategy. Such a strategy could include timing for each entry, pricing structure, level of technological quality expected, and so on.

Not all markets will be ready to accept a new technology at any time. The decision about which market (and territory and specialised group) should be targeted first is a very important strategic decision which requires a great deal of reliable information and expertise of specialist market advisors. Some years back, a well-known car brand presented a small model which was originally aimed for town driving to enable easy parking but for some reason it did not impress the original targeted group of business drivers. It was then, however, discovered that its design, ease of driving, and rear access made it ideal for young mothers ferrying children around. The company promptly offered various bright colours and other design features, and the model became very successful with that target group.

It is exactly for such counterintuitive decisions that a far-sighted researcher entrepreneur relies on good collaborators and partners. Even the best five-star generals rely on the expertise and experience of specialist advisors to ensure a successful campaign.

In Summary

Successful commercialisation depends on many factors, but none are more important than planning, especially strategic planning. Even before setting up the start-up, there are many strategic decisions that need to be taken, such as the correct timing for protection application, for contacting potential partners, for applying for funding, for deciding when in the investment cycle one should start scaling up activities, etc. Many of these will require the advice of specialists, but the final strategic decisions are the entrepreneurs alone.

There Is More than One Way to Rome 11

A successful technological enterprise is built on one or more technologies which offer something that does not exist in the market. It must offer unique added value or special characteristics that users want. Ideally it should address a real need, whether this is expressed, implied, dormant, or latent. The researcher entrepreneur himself or herself may develop a new technology to satisfy a previously identified need, e.g. a sensor or an app. On the other hand, a technology transfer expert (or technology broker) may identify a need and then search for inventions or technologies that, either through adaptation or further development, might address and fulfil this need. Both these approaches are termed "market pull" and represent the bulk of technology transfer cases.

Of course, technology transfer also works the other way around; however, this is generally much more difficult. In this case, a completely new technology is assessed to be promising in general, and a use or application is found for it. This is usually termed "technology push", and although it is rarer, it may eventually form the basis of technological revolutions. The whole microelectronics revolution is based on the discovery of the quirky "transistor" more than 40 years ago.

In the case of market pull, which is by far the most usual motivation for developing a new technology, the target application (i.e. the need) is identified, and a set of technical and functional specifications are drawn up to help with the search or the development. So much is well known and understood. But what is not always appreciated by researchers (and entrepreneurs) is that any industrial or market need can be satisfied by more than one technology, and technological solutions are more often than not in competition with one another.

I personally receive numerous technology requests where an industrial need requires a new material, process, or other technology to satisfy it. More often than not, a number of independent solutions already exist, and these must now be evaluated both against the specifications and against each other. It is often such competition that presents the researcher entrepreneur with the greatest challenge: since other technologies are also vying to be accepted for the same application, you will have to ensure that your technology is developed in such a way that it is assessed to be the best solution for that particular application.

An added complication is that we don't always know the exact conditions that our technology will be used in, even if we are in possession of the specifications. Industry is loath to divulge sensitive information – even when their need is serious – but they expect a good solution regardless. This is where targeted pilot and industrial testing come in. In the TT Guide, I placed great emphasis on the need for the careful design and execution of extensive pilot testing with repeated iterations until the solution is more or less optimal for the application and the technology reaches TRL 6. This, however, is still not enough. Industrial development should then follow with even more stringent and close-to-real conditions of testing, in collaboration with the end-user or implementer. It is the eventual aim that your technology should reach TRL 7 and eventually 8 during this phase of industrial testing.

How, then, is a technology selected among others for a particular application? Apart from the extent to which it fulfils the technological requirements and specifications, the chief aspect that will make your technology stand out from the competition is *cost-benefit ratio*. This is the actual benefit expected to be gained by its use weighed against the total additional investments needed for its industrial development as well as the final price to the user. This is not at all easy to calculate, and many assumptions have to be made in an attempt to get it right. The problem is that it is not easy to compare expected benefits between very different solutions. This is illustrated very well by the difficulty in choosing between different medicines (or medical procedures) for a particular ailment, for example, when all of the solutions on offer result in an array of undesirable side effects, necessitating compromises.

Another good example to illustrate the difficulty in determining *comparable* cost-benefit reliably is the situation encountered when trying to decide on the quality of materials and parts to be used in systems that are designed to have a finite life. I am referring here to the business concept of *planned obsolescence*. This in fact points to an important manifestation of "benefit", the *reliability* of a technology. Simply put, reliability is the average amount of time between failures and is a major determinant of the perceived "quality" and expected lifetime of a technology or product.

Planned obsolescence was introduced in the 1970s in an attempt to cut manufacturing costs in the USA. It was prevalent in many industries such as vehicles, all kinds of devices and instruments, computers, as well as the vast majority of consumer items right up to the 1990s. In most of these cases, the "reasonable expectations of reliability" of the actual target markets were taken into consideration to determine the quality of manufacturing. If the target market was at the top end (i.e. most expensive), then it made sense to use materials and processes that would last well beyond the planned age of the system since the price of the system easily covered the marginally higher manufacturing cost. At the lower end of the market, however, the materials used were themselves at the lower end of the market. This approach served the bottom line of many industries for decades, as attested by the huge environmental impact of millions of discarded cars and consumer items still

11 There Is More than One Way to Rome

visible throughout the industrial world. We'll have more to say on planned obsolescence in Chap. 13, where we will consider fit-for-purpose designing.

This situation, however, underwent a drastic reversal during the last two decades of the twentieth century, much of it due to stronger environmental protection pressures. The widespread tendency for planned obsolescence shifted in response mainly to Japanese (and other) manufacturing practices which routinely use high quality materials and processes for all of their products, irrespective of final cost, thereby increasing the lifetime and reliability of their products substantially. The competitive advantage of such products in terms of quality eventually pulled most manufacturers worldwide in line, and the nett reliability of many systems has increased very substantially. One only has to look at the remarkable increase in the reliability of cars and most types of consumer electronics over the last few decades to be convinced of this. Interestingly, Chinese manufacturing quality, although at the very bottom of many markets at the turn of this century, has shown a rapid (and welcome) tendency to follow the Japanese example and is now challenging the top end of the markets in many sectors, not least of these being consumer electronics, vehicles, and others.

So the selection between various rival technologies for a particular application is based on these three main considerations: satisfaction of technological specifications, technological and functional reliability, and cost-benefit ratio. Once these core considerations are satisfied, a number of other parameters may also be taken into account when selecting between different technologies, depending on the particular situation. For example, a technology may be selected over another one because of the following:

- It is less disruptive to existing operations or "fits in" better in the user company,
- It requires less re-skilling of operators or workers at the user company,
- The cost of servicing it outweighs its higher capital cost,
- It is *perceived* by the potential users as being more "acceptable" or "compatible" with the current customer base of the user company,
- It is *perceived* to be closer to "traditional operating practices", the "values and principles", and the "operating philosophy" of the user company, whatever these may be,
- The technology company (i.e. the start-up) is *perceived* to offer higher capability for long-term support,
- The technology company is *perceived* to offer higher reliability.
- The researcher or inventor has higher *reputation*, etc.

Note that many of the above criteria refer to the *perception* of the technology and the start-up. This perception may not always reflect reality as it depends on the way you have marketed your technology or how the end-user expects it to be.

A final point may be made in relation to the competition. Alternative solutions to a need may even be found in completely different fields, frequently offering good benefit at a low cost. Good examples of successful "spill-over" technological solutions (accidentally or by design) include the use of the Global Positioning

System (GPS originally developed for military and space applications) for everyday tasks such as route mapping or position monitoring; non-stick coatings for cooking pots (originally developed for reduced friction); and the adaptation of fibre-toughening (seen in many biological systems) for the development of tough and strong high temperature ceramic composites for aerospace applications.

In this regard, it is worth remembering the huge benefits that can be obtained from observing physical and biological systems. Such practices of *biomimicry* can help researchers to glean numerous brilliant insights for solving problems, devising new systems, or taking new approaches.

In conclusion, whatever your technology is and however well it addresses a need or fits an application, there is always the possibility that something else will appear to challenge it. Maintaining its competitiveness needs to be seen as a continuous task requiring constant monitoring and evaluation. This is one of the core roles, perhaps the pivotal role, of an entrepreneur.

In Summary

There are often a number of alternatives for solving a technological need, a problem, or a demand. Deciding between them is a systematic exercise, and the final choice will need further development and iteration for optimisation. But even then, there always exists the possibility that a new technology will arise to challenge your choice. Constant monitoring is a major task of the entrepreneur.

Be Disruptive... But Don't Disrupt!   12

Often, you will hear people say that such and such a technology is "disruptive". By this, they mean that it can potentially form the backbone of a new technological revolution by opening up a whole new direction that had not been conceived or foreseen before. It instigates, as it were, a paradigm shift or a radical break with past practices and capabilities. Examples abound in our time: for instance, while mobile telephony had been in the works for many years, many of its eventual uses had not been thought of and it became phenomenally successful when these were tapped – it is certainly a disruptive technology. The Internet is probably the most important example of a disruptive technology, as it instigated the development of a plethora of associated revolutionary products and services, such as email, social networking, electronic shopping, online financial transactions, online dating, etc. Before this technological proliferation, the discovery of the semiconductor was another massively disruptive technological development which ushered in the electronic era during the late 1960s. Calculators, computers, hi-fi sound systems, and many more all followed on from the ripple effect of the new technology.

Going further back in time, there is probably nothing that can compare with the immense impact and scope of the discovery and eventual harnessing of electricity in the nineteenth century, which went on to define the modern world. As a striking example of the influence technologies can have on society, electricity has by far and away been one of the most positively disruptive.

All of these and many more, lesser or greater, disruptive technological discoveries and inventions have shaped the technological world we live in today. In fact, many of them have been the beacons that signposted and serve to label the transition from one era to the next, such as "the Bronze Age", "the Iron Age", and the "Industrial Revolution" of the eighteenth and nineteenth centuries. More recently, we have the "Technological Revolution" (also called the 2nd Industrial Revolution) at the turn of the nineteenth to the twentieth centuries and of course the "Digital Revolution" (the 3rd Industrial Revolution) which is based on the development of digital electronics and still defines our age. At present, the 4th Industrial Revolution is underway which is based on the connectivity, advanced analytics, automation, and

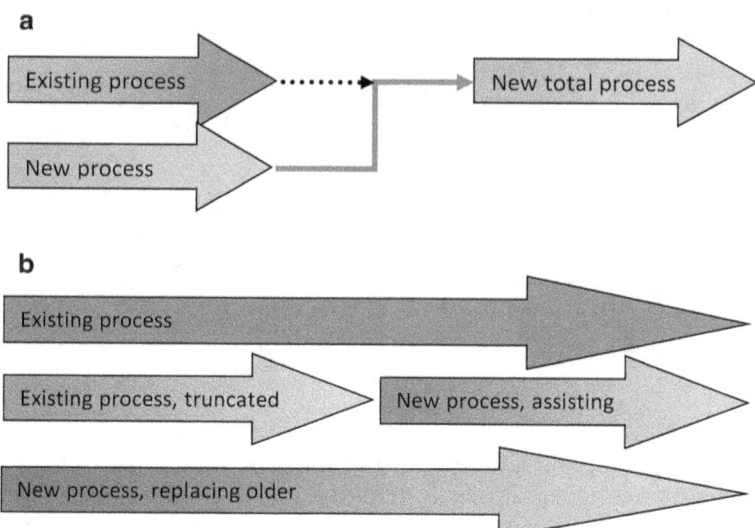

Fig. 12.1 (a) A new process (or device, material, etc.) may be used in parallel with an existing process and gradually replace the existing process. No disruption to operations required. (b) A new process may be included in the production as an assisting process, increasing efficiency and eventually replacing the existing process. No or minimal disruption to operations required

advanced-manufacturing technology which became possible from the proliferation of technologies such as the "Internet of Things" (networked sensors), AI, large database analytics, bio and nano-technologies, 3d printing, etc.

Many smaller or larger disruptive technological developments have changed manufacturing or production by increasing efficiency, reducing cost, or enabling higher quality. In general, therefore, a technological development is said to be disruptive when it succeeds in displacing or replacing an existing technology by virtue of the superior benefits it offers.

If you look closely at these disruptive technologies, however, you will see that none of them succeeded immediately and without hassle; their eventual success relied on their careful, measured, and gradual integration into existing activities, sometimes over many iterations. All of them were first applied in tandem or in parallel with existing technologies and only when they proved their worth did they gradually displace and replace the previous activities. This shows that the successful introduction of a new technology into existing operations depends on whether it can first be used alongside or in tandem with the existing technology as illustrated in Fig. 12.1a, thereby ensuring that the disruption that often occurs when a new technology is introduced to a system is kept to a minimum. Here, a distinction becomes clear between the positive disruptive potential of new technologies that are urgently needed or whose time has come – as in the major examples described above – and the negative disruptive potential of new technologies which might sabotage their entry into the market by affecting existing production practices.

12 Be Disruptive... But Don't Disrupt!

Severe disruption is tolerated in a minority of cases; instead, technologies should aim to disrupt through a process of *integration* as indicated in Fig. 12.1b where a new technology initially assists and gradually displaces the existing one.

All companies hate disruption of their operations, especially when it comes to production. If, then, your technology is to become embedded or integrated into a system which is currently in use, or will require major changes to the way a factory operates, or will cause a disruption in the production process, acceptance may be very difficult since at least some productivity disruption and production stoppage will be required. The same is true for any technology that is aimed at replacing an existing one and which will require adjustment, re-engineering, or other adaptation of existing operations.

On the other hand, acceptance will in theory be easier if your technology is a product or process which requires a whole new production line. This depends however on the acceptance on the part of the implementer that there is a strong need for it in the market or in industry.

Yet again, therefore, the criterion that will determine whether or not your technology is accepted is the benefit to be obtained by making the change weighed against the associated cost. The cost includes both direct – the actual expense involved in developing, adapting and installing the new technology – and indirect cost which could include the cost of disrupting operations, of convincing customers to buy it, of any adverse influence on existing lines of products, and so on.

If, then, operational disruption is inevitable, it should be kept to an absolute minimum. Let's take the example of a small wear-resistant part, produced using a new and better material, that is aimed at replacing an older part in a large system. In order to minimise disruption to operations, the technology provider should design the new part so as to be as functionally similar as possible to the part that it will replace. In fact, he or she could exploit this opportunity to make possible improvements to the part's integration into the system. Keeping disruption to a minimum is central to increasing the potential for acceptance of such technologies in industry and the market.

Disruption, however, is rarely inevitable. Most technologies can usually be redesigned to ensure minimal or no disruption. One should consider carefully all the possible alternative ways of applying the new technology, and after weighing all the pros and cons, select the least disruptive way. Ideally, the only time a disruptive technology should be chosen is when the operations are being upgraded from the ground up or when the liability of continuing with the existing operations is too large to ignore.

Another example may help to illustrate this point. In a mining operation of bentonite, a clay mineral used in oil prospecting, one of the most time-consuming operations is the activation of the ore which is carried out through the addition of a small amount of a chemical and slow heating over as many as 10 days. A new technology based on microwave heating has been designed which speeds up the activation process to only a few minutes, and it can be applied either by replacing the existing activation process or by assisting the existing process. In the first case, productivity would be expected to increase substantially, but it will entail major adjustments to the operations to fit in with the new production method. In the second case, the production method will not change, but the use of a more limited microwave heating stage in series with the existing process means that the productivity increase will be more limited. Which of the two methods would eventually be selected? Even though the immediate benefit is smaller, the second would be chosen, since the disruption would be minimal and allow much easier integration into the existing operations, resulting in better cost-benefit ratio. The added benefit is that the second, less disruptive method will allow safer evaluation and, if positive, at a later stage during major upgrades to the production line, the first approach might then be applied.

Such gradual adaptations are usually possible with most technologies, and one of the most important technological questions you will have to answer during industrial development is exactly this. How do you make sure that your technology will be accepted and integrated easily in existing operations with minimum disruption?

The same applies to retrofitting a new technology onto an existing system. Its application should be as smooth and non-disruptive as possible, whilst offering the maximum possible benefits under the circumstances.

Disruption is such an important consideration for the rapid acceptance of your technology that even small production or other operational disruptions can be enough to put users off from trying it. Your priority, then, should be to design your technology to fit in with existing operations as smoothly as possible. Once your technology has proved itself, it can then be allowed to demonstrate the positive nature of its disruptiveness and resulting benefits in the long run.

In Summary

An industrial partner will always accept to test and further develop a new technology much more amicably if it minimises disruption during the field or pilot testing. But even when it is fully developed, a new innovative technology should be aimed at successful retrofitting into or assisting existing production operations in order to be more easily acceptable, especially in the middle of the investment cycle.

Think Ahead and Fit the Purpose 13

When it comes to technologies and their applicability, one size does not fit all. Even when we are forced to use a technology in order to satisfy a need that it was not originally designed for, we may not always be able to adapt it according to our need. Or, even if the adaptation is possible, it may result in a less than optimum solution which could be frustrating and force a rethink on the part of your potential or actual customers. All in all, technologies that are not designed to be "fit for purpose" are generally wasteful, inefficient, and ineffective.

The crucial aspect here, therefore, is to design from the start and eventually build or adapt your technology to be "fit for the purpose it is intended". In other words, to ensure optimal uptake by users, the technology must be designed – even from the inception stage – to fit the application, no more and no less. We can call this the Goldilocks principle. If a technology is over-designed, it may turn out to be too costly to produce as well as too costly to interest users. On the other hand, if it is under-designed, it may not be functionally satisfactory or even inefficient. I was recently approached by an inventor who was developing a new type of wood-burning water heater. He had identified an area in the heat exchanger where a clever redesign could offer approximately 10–20% improvement in efficiency. The catch was that a cheap way to incorporate this design to existing heaters had to be found so that the cost-benefit ratio would still be favourable. Personally, I was not at all confident that this was possible because special high-temperature resistant materials would be needed which would add a substantial cost. Although the idea was sound, the overall system was over-designed for the purpose. In addition, the performance benefit (added value) was probably too low for the new technology to succeed in this low-end market.

Many cost-sensitive industries battle to balance the cost margin with the benefit margin to achieve the right type of cost-benefit balance even under shifting expectations. This is a further important point: people's expectations shift often, and the point of cost-benefit balance nearly always shifts with them. Such expectation shifts may occur in response to progress, e.g. the technological progress of an application, or in response to external sensitivities, e.g. environmental protection or energy savings, etc. External market influences can also cause shifts in expectations: if, for example, a competitor's new product appears to be "better" than yours, this should generally force a rethink of your own product. While you can follow such shifts and try to remain competitive, there may come a time when you realise that it is not worth pursuing it anymore because the cost-benefit ratio has become prohibitive.

Fit-for-purpose design and manufacturing is important in nearly all industries, and over-design or over-engineering can be costly in other, non-obvious ways as well. In the aeronautics and space industries, for instance, excess weight costs a lot. It has been estimated that every kilogram of material that is put into orbit around the earth costs upwards of 10,000 Euro. There is, then, tremendous benefit to be gained by calculating exact engineering margins and not relying on the usual "a margin of 2 should suffice, let's use 3 to be safe" way of thinking. Such decisions can be extremely costly, especially now that the space industry has become very competitive and is not purely a governmental game anymore, at least in Europe and the USA. The same is true, albeit to a lesser extent, in the aeronautics and even the automobile industries. The latest generation of airplanes is at least 30% more fuel efficient mainly because of the use of lighter materials, e.g. carbon-fibre composites instead of aluminium alloys, as well as improvements in the design and materials of jet turbines. This increase in efficiency is the result of research and development that started in the 1980s and has had a very costly and long development period since, all the while aiming to balance reliability (and performance) with cost. In all of these industries, the trend has been for more and more accurate and reliable modelling so that the design can be determined as accurately as possible from the outset.

Fit-for-purpose designing refers both to functionality and to market position or target market. You should search and consider carefully what exactly any target market wants or needs and why this has not been satisfied yet, before deciding on the final characteristics of your technology. In other words, think ahead before you put pen to paper to develop your technology and its application focus. It will be very difficult to correct your position afterwards. If your technology or product is already on the market, be very careful of rebalancing because users who are used to a particular high level of quality or characteristic will not take lightly to any attempt on your part to "rebalance" cost and benefit. The principle of early cost-performance balanced design will save you a lot of trouble and cost further down the line.

In the automobile industry, fit-for-purpose thinking is very widespread, right down to the quality of the cars, the target market expectations, and the expected lifetime of their components. While one may not agree with applying the principle of fit-for-purpose design at all levels, it does certainly make cost-saving sense in the case of non-critical components – that is, as long as users and customers do not perceive it as an attempt on your part to short-change them. Any negative change in the quality or functionality level of your technology for the sake of balancing your books can work against you. By way of illustration, a well-known market leader in the European automotive industry tried during the late 1990s to reduce costs by using slightly lower quality materials and components. Whereas they thought that they were still safely within their cost-benefit balance range, their attempt backfired as their customers had become used to higher levels of quality and quickly turned away when they realised that this had been reduced. The company has since reversed its decision, but only after suffering serious damage to its reputation. More than 15 years hence, it still has not recovered its market position as the top Japanese brands jumped in very quickly emphasising their reliability and quality and filled many niches.

On the other hand, during the last century, several automobile companies (mainly American) contrived to sharpen the principle of fit for purpose by developing the idea of "planned obsolescence" – a very successful tactic which has since become very widespread in many industries for consumer goods. As we discussed before, the rationale for this strategy was based on the premise that since an average car would be replaced every 6 years or so, it made sense to design them to last for only that length of time! From the point of view of the environment of course, it is a great pity that other manufacturers capitalised on the "success" of this strategy by imitating it and started to design and build cars that didn't last as long as before. From a purely profit-based point of view, though, it made perfect cost-benefit sense for these companies at the time. The widespread adoption of "planned obsolescence" strategies notwithstanding, there is a clear trend nowadays to reverse this attitude since manufacturers are now expected by law (in Europe, Japan and the US at least) to cover the cost of the whole life of a product (including the cost of recycling). This has made it less expensive overall to produce a good quality long-lasting car than one that will need to be replaced after only a few years. In the long run however, all such companies have paid a price by losing reputation, and all of them have lost global market positions.

Finally, a few words about intelligent and self-adapting technologies. The latest trend of designing and building intelligent systems (which have a plethora of sensors and actuators built in, hence the "intelligent" or "smart" moniker) allows for a reduction of overall cost by designing in a capability of the system to adapt and tune itself to specific applications. Some such technologies already exist and others are in the pipeline. All of these technologies promise to be "fit for many purposes" by adjusting themselves to varying environmental or operational conditions. Some of these include intelligent coatings and facades for buildings, cars that can adjust their operational parameters according to conditions, self-optimising embedded systems for the delivery of medicines, and so on. It's a sign of things to come where many of our safety-related and other critical decisions will be made for us.

The latest attempts at introducing self-driving cars in cities is an interesting case in point here. While they are already quite ubiquitous in certain cities such as San Francisco in the USA (mainly taxis and cabs), they have not yet convinced the market that they have a real future as consumer cars. The main reason, I believe, is that they have no clear purpose or large target market in the general consumer sector.

Apart from the actual technical problems leading to quite a few accidents due to misreading the environment or human drivers' or pedestrians' responses, there is a major question about liability. Who is to pay when a self-driving car is involved in such an accident due to a technical error or technical inadequacy on the part of the "driving" computer? This is the reason that all such cars (except cabs, under strict conditions) cannot be advertised as such, but a human driver must always keep eyes on the road and be ready to take over, defeating the original idea. In addition, there seems to be a strong resistance developing against 24 hour self-driving cars with a number of easy defeat tricks being used to freeze them. All in all, I believe the only major application of such self-driving cars will remain in the military (air or land or sea drones, etc.) and perhaps in guarded and constrained mass transport, as already existing in various airports and certain tram lines.

In Summary

The most successful technologies are always designed carefully from the start to "fit" exactly the purpose they are expected to satisfy. Technologies that are not designed to be "fit for purpose" are generally wasteful, inefficient, and ineffective. There is no point in designing a car where the engine will outlast the chassis by 20 years or vice versa. A technology needs to be at the "Goldilocks" level: just right.

Is Your Financial Base Solid? 14

Building a new enterprise, however small, can be an expensive decision. In addition to the normal legal, administrative, and other expenses, you'll have to make sure you are financially covered for the whole initial period when you are still testing your technology and building your company and sales will be weak or non-existent. The length of this period is very difficult to estimate of course, so it's better to be conservative in your calculations and your use of cash.

But before we look at the various expenses and potential sources of funding, a word of warning: it is very easy to overspend, especially at the beginning, while you are building the foundations of your company, so you have to be extremely diligent in working out and keeping to your spending plan. Every expense must be very carefully thought out with the two crucial criteria being: "do we absolutely need this now?" and "how does this expense fit into our detailed development plan?". In particular, avoid all expenses that do not offer a specific and clear benefit to your plans, be they technical or otherwise. I have seen very promising start-ups being weighed down with unnecessary expenses right at the start, which later on proved to be a major handicap and contributed to failure. Examples of unnecessary expenses are new offices, (where an existing office and labs could suffice), company cars, trips for meeting potential collaborators before ascertaining their clear interest or need for the technology, patent expansion into unnecessary territories, employing new staff before ascertaining clear needs, production equipment for very small test batches (where manual production could easily suffice), and so on.

Let us now see what kind of expenses you should expect at the start of your company's life and how you could try to reduce them or even avoid them. They can take the following form:

- *Legal and administrative fees and taxes.* The initial costs of setting up your company vary widely from country to country. The trend during the last 10 years has been to reduce bureaucratic hassles in many countries, especially in the European Union, but some costs can still be substantial. For example, even though the recently established "European Limited Liability Company" can be set up with only 1 Euro of capital (which reduces various associated fees), in reality you should estimate the company capital to reflect the minimum inelastic expenses your company will be expected to have over the first 12 months or so. This should include rents, basic salaries, utilities (electricity, water, telephone...), etc. If you don't do this and you need to raise the company capital later, it is often more expensive.

In most cases you can set up your company without the assistance of a lawyer. For example, personal companies do not need dedicated legal support, beyond the initial advice. However, Company Articles need to be prepared very carefully reflecting the correct legal status, and you will soon require legal documents to aid your negotiations with potential adopters of your technology. These include but are not limited to Memoranda of Understanding (MoU), Non-Disclosure Agreements (NDA, also called Confidentiality Agreement), Licensing Agreements, Technology Transfer Agreements, and others (see also the next chapter). All of these documents need to be prepared properly in order to obtain the maximum protection and cover from them, and therefore, obtaining the services of a good lawyer with experience in commercial law in your country (and internationally) would be a very good idea. You will find a discussion of such issues and realistic samples of many of the above documents in the TT Guide as well as on many advisory services in the internet.

- *Accounting services* will be needed at all times during the life of a company. Most countries require that Limited Liability (Ltd), GmbH, or Société Anonyme (SA) type companies must employ the services of an accountant who will be legally responsible for keeping the books, attending to taxation requirements and demands, filing tax returns, etc. In most cases, a start-up company will probably be able to use the services of an accountant on an *ad hoc* basis, thereby much reducing costs.

   An accountant is also essential for the day-to-day running of the new company since you will not have the time to keep up with the changes in financial regulations that occur frequently in many countries.

- *Rents and other associated expenses* will probably be one of the largest outlays you will have if you decide that you absolutely need new offices and laboratories. As mentioned, these should be generally avoided or substantially reduced until the company is well established and has started turning an income. For a start, consider whether you actually need offices. For example, if your technology is mainly computer-based, then perhaps you can set up your company at home and expand later from there. And if your technology is a direct off-shoot from a laboratory, you could have your company offices (legal address) at home while you continue your development in a protected (confidential) corner of the laboratory. On the other hand, many universities and research centres have built "Technology Parks" (TP) and "Incubators" where start-up companies can be housed for the first few years without any of the accompanying hassle. There are many advantages to such a solution since the costs are generally lower, and you will have access to substantial technical and non-technical support in or near the TP or Incubator.

- *Intellectual property (IP) protection and dissemination expenses* need to be taken into account as well, as these can be very substantial. While initial filing for patent protection or IP recognition in your country's Patent Office is inexpensive (in the region of 50-100 Euro), if you decide to pursue strong patenting protection, then the associated expenses can increase dramatically. These costs will be in addition to the maintenance fees (which increase substantially over the 20 years' life of a patent). For example, filing at the European Patent (EP) office currently costs in the region of 2500 Euro (excluding any legal costs), and the awarding cost would set you back another 500 Euro or so. The Patent Cooperation Treaty (PCT) allows for a common filing for almost all remaining countries, and the filing cost is similar, but you need to translate your patent for every language you are considering which is a very expensive proposition.

My advice is to file in your country initially and then decide later whether you want to attempt EP or PCT filing for the countries where you are expecting to market (a patent protects in the countries where it is awarded). I say this because a strategy that many inventors follow is to file for a patent early in order to obtain proof of date of invention and keep others from using the technology, thereby enabling the inventor's freedom for use. This also allows time for evaluation and decision-making regarding the potential of the technology. A number of my own patents have exactly this purpose since a publication does *not* stop a competitor from adapting the technology and then patenting it for a different application.
- *Marketing and dissemination* is almost always the most important aspect of developing a market presence and sales. Unless your technology's customers are few and you already have established strong contacts with them (as happens for example in a few very niche industries such as parts of space or defence markets), it is most important to talk about your technology or product in open fora such as conferences, fairs, and exhibitions. There is nothing wrong with mentioning your new technology or product in a scientific paper, giving the patent number, etc. Specialised conferences and symposia also offer many opportunities for presenting your new technology to an interested audience and even exhibit it. The Internet of course offers extensive opportunities for focused marketing, and you should make the most of it through search engines and the creation of a dedicated website for your technology, social media, and so on.
- *Technical costs* particular to your technology, such as licensing fees for supporting technologies, further research and development costs, costs for demonstrations and exhibitions, samples, particular adaptations to specific markets, etc.
- *Other expenses* in support of your technology and enterprise such as travelling, publications and brochures, translations, and others.

All of the above can add up to very substantial amounts. They need to be detailed and explained in your business plan and you should keep to your expense plan as much as possible. Therefore, adequate financial support must be secured before you take the big step.

So the big question is: where can you find adequate financial support?

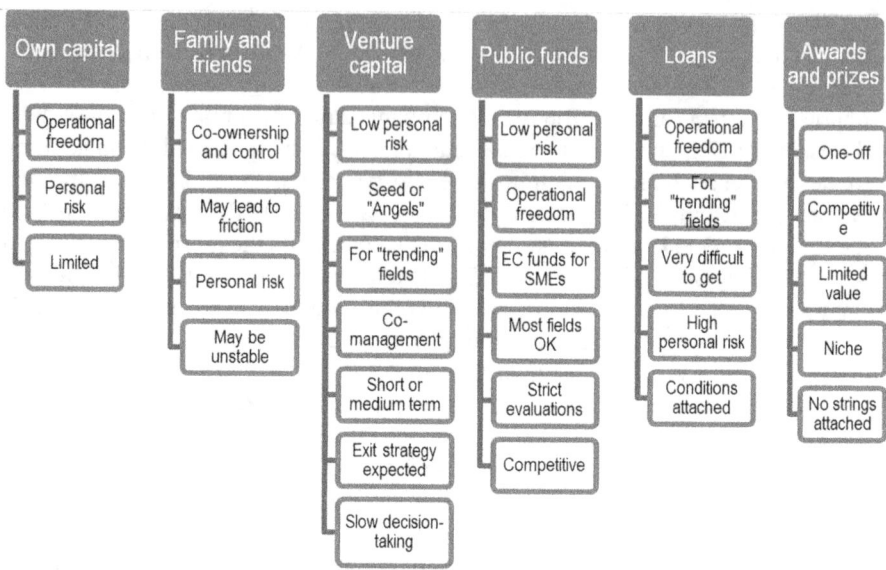

Fig. 14.1 Various funding sources available for start-ups and associated issues

There are many sources of funding although not all of them are applicable in every case and many come with conditions, as summarised in Fig. 14.1. Apart from depending on your own (and family's or friends' money), you have a choice of a number of funding bodies that would be willing – after a strict evaluation – to fund your enterprise. Let's consider them in turn.

All sources for start-up funding have advantages and disadvantages:

- If you decide to use **your own money** to set up and run the start-up, you probably can expect both the best and worst of worlds. It is still the most frequent source of funds for a start-up and the one that allows you freedom of movement and decision-making, but it also means the maximum amount of risk if your start-up does not succeed. If this is your choice, then make sure you calculate all expenses as accurately as possible to ensure that you have enough to see you through the initial stages till income starts flowing.
- Funds from **friends or family** are another source of private money, but in this case, you only have partial freedom of operations and decision-making. If you also put your own money, then you still have a personal risk if things don't work out. The main problem with this route is one of trust. Unless you get your backers to accept your better judgment regarding the development of your technology and the running of the new company, collaborating with friends or family may lead to friction and problems. In the worst case, such instability can affect the development of the company and lead to the break-up of the collaboration. In one case I recall, a young entrepreneur had received funding from a family friend to develop some promising industrial security software (developed during his MSc work),

but market difficulties led to long delays (over a year) in launching and cost overruns. This led to arguments and irritation on the part of his relative backer who stopped funding and insisted on getting his money back immediately. Fortunately, the software was completed soon after and the young company managed to sell an exclusive license with which it paid back the original backer. I believe the company is still in operation with another product in the pipeline, but it could easily have gone the other way.

- **Venture Capital** (VC) firms are a widespread (especially in the USA, China, and Japan) potential source of funding, but they generally prefer to invest in what they perceive as low-risk areas such as informatics (new software, games, apps, etc.), energy production, or medical technologies where they (currently) estimate that the corresponding markets are very strong and bullish. These preferred areas can change in the future as markets shift and change. While VCs do not exclude other, not-so-bullish areas, they generally have a short-to-medium investment horizon and expect a return of at least 30–50% over 3 years after which they expect to exit. They can demand a large chunk of the ownership (once I was offered a deal of 85% for the VC and 15% for me on the grounds that my technology was too risky – I did not accept) and co-management. Although your particular personal risk is low, business decisions are mostly made by the VC's appointed managers and can be slow and not always in the direction you might wish to go.

VCs can sometimes be useful for very early-stage financing when (limited, usually not more than about 300k Euro) "seed" financing by investment "angels" can help with the technology demonstration costs, before or soon after a company is formed. In this case, the conditions are less strict and demanding, and the decisions may be quicker while funding may be available for a wider range of fields.

- Many countries nowadays offer **public grants** to help start-ups on their way. The funds may be 100% public or the authorities may expect a like-to-like contribution (30–50%), especially from existing companies. They are generally competitive and you need to submit well-argued proposals. Funded projects are always monitored.

Within the framework of the current European Union's RD "Horizon" Programmes, in addition to very substantial research funding in many areas, there are two sub-programmes focused on helping new start-ups, the "SME Instrument" and "Access to Risk Finance". Whereas the former funds 100% of either preparatory activities (Stage A, up to 50k Euro to prepare a Business Plan) or actual industrial and business development of the start-up (Stage B, up to 1.5M Euro), the latter is a finance-guarantee instrument for later activities. Other similar programmes are also available for industrial development, e.g. the long-running Eureka programme and others. Lately, the "Smart Specialisation" platform within the structural funding programme aims at enhancing the competitiveness of companies at the regional level throughout the European Union. All of the above are competitive programmes with varying possibility for success (anything from 10 to 50%). More information can be found online as well as in the TT Guide.

- You may be able to obtain a **loan** from a bank or other financial institution. While these carry the biggest personal risk for you (interest rates are generally higher than the inflation rate), they may offer important bridging finance to take you over a difficult patch. You should only consider taking a loan if you are sure your start-up is going to be successful, if this is ever possible. For this reason, a loan should only be taken once some income source has been identified and customer orders are clearly in the pipeline.
- Finally, a number of interesting new funding instruments have recently appeared, offering **awards** (sometimes substantial) and/or **prizes** for solving specific technological problems. They are all run by technology brokerages and two of the most well-known are "NineSigma™" and "Innocentive™", both based in the USA. They work by placing international calls for solutions (to subscribers) to very specific problems in all fields, and the awards are made after evaluation. IP rights may be expected to be transferred, but this is not obligatory.

All of the above financing routes have pros and cons and not all will work in every case. The decision on which route you'll take is yours, but you should always keep in mind the possibility that your start-up might not work out. Remember that setting up a start-up is risky so you should always try to minimise the associated risks. One way of doing this is to apply to multiple funding bodies and hope for the best.

In Summary

Attempting to set up a start-up company without making sure your financial base is solid (or potentially so) is dangerous and potentially lethal. There are many more expenses involved during the first year than during the later years, and all of them need to be covered as early as possible. The challenge is that all sources of funding have pros and cons and most have conditions attached. A mixed bag of funding sources is probably safer, but getting too much funding can easily lead to serious problems in a short time.

In... Agreements We Trust

A business is always founded on legal grounds and relies on various legal frameworks for it to develop and flourish. You will be expected to sign many agreements – purchasing, supply, funding, etc. – and all will have legal repercussions. This is not completely unlike the various research contracts that you may have had to sign to carry out your research work, which generally lay out the framework of the work you are expected to carry out (i.e. the objectives) and the deliverables expected from you at the end of the day. The main difference is that a research effort may or may not be successful and produce a competitive technology or product, but life will go on as before, most of the time, whereas a business needs to sell to survive. The critical difference is that a business contract is legally binding – that is, you are *binding* yourself to provide such and such technology or product or service to the customer, and if you don't (or can't), you will probably have to shoulder the consequences, financial penalty, or even the failure of your start-up. In other words, business agreements always have serious legal repercussions which must never be taken lightly.

To safeguard yourself and your business, all your transactions should be based on legally binding agreements which must be carefully prepared, preferably by a legal expert. In actual fact, the most successful businesses are characterised by their emphasis on ensuring that nearly all inputs and outputs are protected by some sort of contract or licensing agreement.

Let's consider supplier-customer agreements. There are many different types of inputs used by technological companies: supplies (machinery, consumables, utilities, etc.), personnel, information, technological know-how, and others. Nearly all such supplies cost money so their relative importance and potential added value need to be evaluated before signing off any agreements for their supply. Such evaluation can take many forms, but the overriding consideration is trust. Just as the value of a currency note (i.e. cash) relies on our trust that the bank will honour its commitment to "pay the bearer" the amount written on the note, so do all our transactions with suppliers (and customers) rely on mutual trust, and they are underlined by legally binding contracts, whenever necessary. Naturally, you, as a supplier will also be called upon to sign and honour agreements with your customers.

Many types of agreement are necessary in business, but all have a number of aspects in common:

- A preamble where the parties to the agreement are identified
- An introduction where the parties' interests and common objectives in pursuing the agreement are presented
- The main body of the agreement where various clauses lay out the details of the agreement, including any non-disclosure clauses
- The legal framework and legal background to the agreement
- The signatures by the official representatives of the parties

In some cases, agreements need to be witnessed by a legal counsel or other persons, but in most cases, this is not necessary and the signatures of the officially designated signatories of each party are sufficient. Nearly all countries allow such personal agreements to be considered as legally binding in nearly all cases. The idea is to reduce bureaucratic burden on business as far as is practicable.

A word of warning at this point: no amount of legal or personal agreements can replace common sense, especially in business. Just as you would not consider the word of a personal adversary as trustworthy and binding, so you should not expect the word of a conman to be worth anything, no matter how many signed agreements you may conclude. In all your transactions, exercise common sense: check and cross-check all potential associates by carrying out a careful search (the Internet is a wonderful aid in this regard, but do be aware of false leads and misinformation) and enquire with associates, even bankers and customers. A due diligence report is often necessary in cases of large and critical agreements, especially with suppliers. Only after you have eliminated all possible causes for concern to a satisfactory level should you consider signing an agreement.

Now, let's look at some of the agreements you will deal with when you set up your start-up. The very first agreement you will probably conclude is a memorandum of understanding (MoU), perhaps with your own company partners or a business partner. A MoU is essentially an "agreement to discuss a potential business association" which clarifies the conditions under which negotiations can be initiated before a full agreement can be signed. Its general structure is similar to that of a full agreement, but the MoU only contains the preamble and the introduction with only 1 to 2 other clauses, most notably a non-disclosure clause to ensure that discussions are as open as possible without any concerns about confidentiality. MoUs can be used frequently during the life of a company, such as in the following cases:

- Before starting negotiations with partners to set up the company
- Before any discussions regarding the transfer of a technology to or from another entity
- Before a major decision to supply or be supplied by another entity

- Before any discussions on accepting a new partner or funding opportunity with repercussions on the company's operations
- Other major decisions such as marketing or funding drives

MoUs are very useful in many respects as they can help you to determine early on whether a certain venture is worth pursuing, before you commit yourself too deeply. For example, if you would like to transfer your technology to industry, but you don't know if the prospective adopter (the recipient of the technology) offers the best opportunities, the MoU allows you to enter into preliminary discussions and delve deeper into the actual intentions of your prospective partner. In this way, you can always pull out if you are not satisfied, without incurring any loss. A MoU also allows for misunderstandings to be resolved before any commitment is made. In one example I recall, a young post-doc researcher was approached by a small company to work together to develop a new electronic product for the medical sector, based on a process he was working on. During the preliminary discussions (after signing an MoU), the post-doc only then became aware that ownership of the process was actually shared by an earlier researcher who had also contributed to the process and therefore was also invited to be involved.

The MoU also allows time for an early evaluation of the cost-benefit ratio that parties can expect from a collaboration and thrash out ways in which any collaboration can be optimised. All aspects of the potential collaboration need to be discussed during this period, from the level of the technology and its prospects to future plans and directions. Both sides need to feel comfortable during these early negotiations, and both need to believe that they will have something to gain from it, i.e. you should aim to bring about a "win-win" situation for all concerned.

Once the background has been suitably agreed on, with reference to the MoU and the associated discussions, you will be ready to proceed to a full contract. Details of various contracts have been discussed in the TT Guide, and at this point, it is enough to emphasise that successful entrepreneurship is heavily dependent on the care that you take in preparing the various agreements, especially at the outset.

Other types of agreements include those binding personnel working on sensitive projects of your company. Generally, those include details of his or her work contract but also must include specific confidentiality clauses and even various restrictions on working for direct competitors after leaving.

Before wrapping up this chapter, it is worth discussing IP licensing-in and licensing-out agreements. Once your company is up and running, the two main types of agreement that you will need are those that refer to suppliers and those that refer to customers. A special case of the former will be your technology providers since more often than not you will need supporting technologies to get your own technology on the road. If such supporting technologies are protected (i.e. proprietary), you will need to license them in in order for you to use them. This is what happens with many integrated products such as mobile telephones, which depend on many technologies that are owned by third parties. In a recent example that has been brought to my attention, a researcher developed a new material for a high-gain microwave antenna, but he had to licence in the process for making it (an advanced coating process) in order to be able to market it openly.

In the same vein, you need to keep a lookout for anyone needing one of your own technologies which you could benefit from by licensing it out. Although occasionally manufacturers may (innocently, we'd like to believe) attempt to use a proprietary technology without acquiring the rights through a licence, it is generally not worth cheating. If you find out that someone is using your technology, you can demand compensation and (generally) a share of any sales or profits, even if you haven't contributed anything in the industrial development phase. You are completely within your rights to do so, so you should keep your eyes open for any potential infringement or unlicensed usage of your technologies.

All in all, an entrepreneur should see agreements as one of the foundations of a successful enterprise. Even though they entail some expense, they provide a certain level of safeguard for the future development of the company and therefore are certainly worth every penny.

In Summary

All transactions in business (should) involve legal agreements which clarify the exact conditions and background upon which you will base the collaboration. Even at the very start of any potential collaboration, a letter of intent and/or a memorandum of understanding (with attached non-disclosure agreement) will ensure clarity of intentions and purpose from both sides so you can negotiate and agree on all basic conditions and premises freely and without anxiety. In business, no one should be exempt from such agreements: neither relatives nor best friends.

Timing Is Critical 16

It is very rare indeed that a new enterprise succeeds by offering a service or product similar to one that is already successful and well known in the same market. If you try to enter a satisfied market at the wrong time, you will battle to be accepted. The challenge therefore is to identify the exact timing and precise target market – that is, when and where a new product or technology will be well received.

Novelty and innovativeness are paramount for success. As a researcher, you are already aware of the criticality of novelty in your work to ensure success. A publication is not worth the paper it's printed on if it is not novel and does not address a new material, process, method, etc. Not only that, but it must also be published before anyone else's similar results are! A researcher's career is often determined by his or her capability to identify such novelty, to work towards elucidating it, and to publish it at the opportune time.

It is the same with a successful enterprise. If you are determined to be a successful researcher entrepreneur, you will succeed only if you have something new and significantly different to offer and if you offer it at the right time and to the right market. But what does this mean in practice and how can you ensure that you are ready to take the initiative to bring your new technology to the market?

The short answer is, as always, obvious in retrospect: you are ready to enter a particular market if your technology or product or service addresses a specific need or demand *at this point in time*! To succeed in this therefore, a close market watch is crucial. By watching the market or markets and "listening" to the needs and demands being expressed (indeed, sometimes "below the surface"), you will know when to move. Entering the market at the wrong time may not only be disastrous financially but it may also have a negative effect on your reputation and, as a consequence, make it very difficult to change market perceptions later.

The critical nature of market entry timing means that your technology or product must be ready well in advance and kept continually updated in readiness for an opportunity to enter the market. You should continue to improve it and even diversify its potential uses as you wait for the right moment. By diversifying its potential applicability, you will have a greater possibility to find a market ready to accept your product.

Let us consider some examples to clarify these points. Over the past few decades, many technologies that address environmental or energy-saving issues have unfortunately failed to be successful due to the absence of environmental safeguards or regulations. For instance, the various technologies for electric or hybrid cars have been well developed since the 1980s but only during the past 10 years or so has there been a much more serious push towards mainstreaming them. This has mainly been the result of a regulatory push by various states (especially some American states, notably California, as well as states in the European Union) which have encouraged alternative energy sources for transport by insisting on lower or even zero direct emissions. In the same vein, electricity generation using renewable sources (especially wind and solar panels) has only recently become financially sensible for the same reasons as well as because of the strengthened perception that gas and petrol imports are becoming more and more unstable (both economically and regarding supply). Even so, renewable sources of electricity have only actually taken hold as a result of direct intervention by governments in the form of subsidies and regulatory support, sometimes against strong lobbying from vested interests from, e.g. fossil fuel companies. That, then, was clearly an opportune time for new technologies based on renewable energy sources to be brought into the market, and this fertile period is still very much in evidence today.

In general, therefore, keeping a lookout for a good window of opportunity may be the only way to introduce your technology into a market where powerful vested interests (as for example exist in the case of energy generation in the form of the coal and gas lobbies) would not otherwise allow any new technologies to gain a foothold.

An interesting case that is driven mainly by legislation is that of electric vehicles. It is not very well known that all the basic technologies for electric motor-powered cars have been around for over a century. At the beginning of the nineteenth century, electric cars already held the land speed record! But their heavy and low energy batteries meant that, when internal combustion engines were properly developed and entered the market, they had no chance. Petrol (or diesel) has very high energy density and is still plentiful, so the only way to reduce climate-damaging vehicle emissions is by forcing the gradual withdrawal of all internal combustion engine vehicles. Currently, the (re)introduction of electric vehicles is accelerating, especially because of the advent of high energy density batteries, high powered motors, and renewable electricity generation.

On the basis of such major developments as the forced shift in energy generation routes and electric vehicles, discussed above, a plethora of supporting technologies have found fertile ground to grow and be successful within the window of opportunity that these shifts provided and still provide. For example, the move to renewable energy generation methods has brought a host of advanced materials, electronic sensors, controls, and actuators into the market which hitherto did not have any reasonable grounds for their existence.

Despite the seeming golden window of opportunity opened up by the drive for clean energy, however, even here success may not be guaranteed. At this moment in time, electric cars still remain far from well-established as mainstream transport for a variety of reasons, chief among these being the current slump in the price of petrol, the still less than satisfactory battery charging period and limited range between charges, and the lack of an extensive-enough network of charging points in most major urban areas. The technological challenges among these obstacles open up further opportunities for research and the development of marketable solutions to address them, but unforeseen events are problematic because one cannot plan for them in any way.

A question thus arises: if unforeseen developments can present obstacles even on what appear to be excellent windows of opportunity, does the question of timeliness become nothing more than a question of luck? Hardly. As technologies and technological capabilities progress, the market perception (and that of the public in general) is gradually shifting toward the inevitability of technological development and technological solutions, especially as regards the environment, energy, communication, security, etc. As a result, technology providers continuously "test the ground" by allowing limited releases of new technologies while utilising the waiting time to continue refining their technologies in order for them to be ready for the right opportunity.

The existence of a well-established technological foundation or background is another important consideration regarding the right time to enter a market. There exist several examples of technologies which were successfully introduced into their markets only after enabling technologies became well established. For example, MMS (Multimedia Messaging Service) capability in early mobile telephones never caught on because of the expense involved and the slow download speeds available. When smartphones became ubiquitous, however, media communication services with similar capabilities became possible and have expanded very widely since.

In industry, rapid construction of metallic panel structures became possible only when very powerful cordless electric screwdrivers became available which also pushed the development of associated technologies such as high strength screws, specially prepared panels, etc. To support such a development, new batteries, new fast chargers, and new powerful compact motors were also developed and became available widely. The noteworthy aspect here is that many of these technologies had been more or less ready beforehand (probably at TRL 4-5), but their market applicability only became feasible when someone came up with self-tapping high-strength screws for metallic panels, another enabling technology for rapidly building metallic panel structures.

In the field of computing, manufacturers tend to follow each other's initiatives and bring out new technologies almost in the form of a computing "arms race". While most early computers were perfectly satisfactory for ordinary word processing, Internet, and similar tasks, they soon proved completely inadequate for "heavy" computer gaming or modelling and simulation programmes that were in high demand and gradually became the norm. As a direct response, the demand for greater computing power immediately pushed the development and availability of much more powerful machines which allowed the development of ever more realistic computer simulations, graphics, and games which very soon required even more powerful machines and so on. In the future, it seems safe to say that we'll be looking at today's powerful machines and wonder how on Earth we could have managed with such weaklings.

The important thing to note here is that both sides of this "arms race" could have introduced many of these more advanced technologies (machines or programmes) at almost any time before the need actually arose. It would not, however, have made any business sense since they would not be addressing a pressing need or opportunity. Both sides introduced each new technological step only when it made good business sense and of course when it would allow them to reap the benefits gradually and over as long a period of time as possible.

A much bigger arms race of course is the real one: that of the development of weapons and corresponding technologies to counteract or defend against them. In this area, push-pull dependency is very clear and has been going on for millennia. Timing of the introduction of new technologies is extremely sensitive and always kept secret (as much as possible). Again, it only pays to introduce a new technology when the timing is right so as to avoid spurring the other side on. The current war in Ukraine has established the critical role of drones both for reconnaissance and for attacking by air and sea.

In practice however, it isn't at all easy to decide when the time is "right" to introduce a technology into the market or to offer your technology to industry or to set up a start-up for commercialisation. While technology and market watching yields a lot of useful information, other, non-tangible information is also necessary. For example, market fatigue (especially for a consumer product, but for certain industrial products too) sets in much quicker nowadays than it used to be, and trends (or fads) tend to come and go in a flash. Because marketing ploys set very high expectations, consumers tend to expect new "more developed" products in a cycle of every few months (or even less, in the case of apps and similar products). If a decision to enter a market is delayed for any reason, it could easily happen that a product is introduced after the window of opportunity has closed to the detriment of the supplier.

The state of the general economy and that of the particular sector is another important indicator of timing. Generally, economies tend to be cyclical and industries look to enhance their operations or repair their facilities with new sensors, actuators, and so on before the end of an economic downturn so as to catch the next wave. Consumers' spending power can also be influenced by the state of the economy, for example their willingness or ability to get the newest technological innovation can be influenced by economic downturns.

As mentioned previously, major changes to industrial facilities such as more advanced machinery, new materials, new processes, and methods would only be accepted when a factory is planning its new investment cycle. Your job is to observe and prepare for and anticipate the next wave which you should be ready to ride at a moment's notice. A related situation is presented by many technologies that are aimed at intermediate stages in manufacturing, e.g. processes, materials, or parts. In these cases, "right timing" will be dictated by long-term public trends. Many technologies for protection of the environment, renewable energy generation, and energy saving have found their market relevance recently even though they were developed decades ago. The same is valid for technologies for space exploration whose very long-term planning needs require technological readiness well in advance.

Having said all that, in some cases, the "right moment" may never occur, because the market is already satisfied with existing technologies. In this case, an early (and risky) push into a market may bring benefits, but this is still the exception that proves the rule. For example, electric cars are already very impressive technologically, and their makers have forged a good business case, but they are nonetheless still struggling for wider financial success beyond a narrow medium or high-end market. This is mainly because the market is still saturated with fossil-burning vehicles which exert an undue influence on the public's perceptions and expectations.

The right timing in business is as important as it is in research. A clear and extensive market watch is as crucial for success as it is in science. While the early bird may or may not catch the worm, the bird that waits patiently, keeps a watchful eye on developments, and grabs opportunities at just the right time will stand a very strong chance of being rewarded.

In Summary

In business, timing is very important, but when setting up a start-up, timing is critical. Your technology or product or service should address a specific need or demand *at that point in time*! For this, a close market watch is crucial. By watching the market or markets and "listening" to the needs and demands being expressed (indeed, sometimes "below the surface"), you will know when to move. Entering the market at the wrong time may not only be disastrous financially but it may also have a negative effect on your reputation and, as a consequence, make it very difficult to change market perceptions later.

Risk Wisely 17

You can't make an omelette without breaking eggs. Likewise, you can't win as an entrepreneur unless you are willing to take *well researched, calculated,* and *weighed* risks. This means that since all business ventures have risks associated with them, one of your preparatory activities as an aspiring entrepreneur should include a detailed study of all potential risks, as well as clear identification, as early as possible, of the means and solutions to manage these risks, i.e. the means to minimise them or mitigate them.

As discussed in detail in the TT Guide, a (non-technical) risk is defined as any situation which may have an adverse effect on the objectives and aims of a commercialisation attempt. There are many different types of risk associated with a new business venture, including technological risks, market risks, and financial risks. The likelihood and potential impact of these risks varies according to the type of commercialisation route you choose as well as the specifics of your technology vis-à-vis the industry, market, or sector you are targeting. As an aspiring entrepreneur, you need to carry out a detailed risk analysis *before you set up your company* so that you can determine whether the main risks can be mitigated or controlled and how. In fact, if those risks that are judged to be critical do not lend themselves to any mitigation, it may be advisable to rethink the whole venture.

And this is the sticking point. The transition from research to the market is fraught with difficulties and obstacles and scored through with unknowns. It is not at all straightforward to identify in advance all the situations that may present risks during the life of a new enterprise and certainly not easy to work out solutions to them if you are not aware of them in detail. While this catch-22 situation is difficult to resolve, you should in any case (probably) have some strong indications as to how to move forward. Let us consider some of the most critical risks that you may have to face as a researcher entrepreneur and what you can do about them.

The first and foremost risk to commercialisation is a weak, unresponsive, or even hostile market for your technology. If there is no need or demand for your technology, now or in the foreseeable future, there is simply no point in going ahead with the venture. Of course, it's always possible that the technology may be "ahead of its time" or that there is no enabling technology to make it usable yet or some other *extraneous* reason for which you can do little about at this time and it's better to wait for a more opportune time.

But a further major reason – about which you can probably do something – for market negativity is the *perception* that the public may have regarding your technology. The oft-encountered perceived danger of microwave heating of food – against all evidence to the contrary – is a good example of this. Strangely, microwaves are also implicated in another scare related to mobile phone use, without any scientific evidence of dangers whatsoever. There is little beyond public education that one can do to mitigate such scare-mongering or fake information spreading.

If market negativity is a risk factor, a good mitigating route would be to develop the technology as far as practicable, keep it updated, and wait for an opportune time when the market will require it or is ready to accept its benefits so that your market entry will be well received. There are many major examples where uncertain market acceptance was an obstacle to commercialisation early on. Electric cars, life-like computer games, and renewable energy generation are major examples that spring to mind, but many other, more obscure, technologies have been delayed on purpose so that they could enter the market at a time that it was ready for them. These include various types of polymers that were perceived to be unsuitable but are now used widely at home, microwavable packaged dinners, plastic-bottled water, traceable smart phones, and others.

In the case where a technology is so novel that the public cannot form an opinion on it or needs to be informed of its capabilities (or at least gently coerced to consider it), an extensive marketing campaign may create a market need or demand for it. This is a popular route that manufacturers use (especially manufacturers of consumer electronics) to promote a new product or technology that is facing natural resistance and may even require governmental permission for its introduction. Currently, self-driving cars and home-help robots are being presented and debated widely in various media in order to test public acceptance and judge the best time for their mass introduction.

Beyond market acceptance, a second very important aspect which may present serious risks to the commercialisation of a technology is inadequate level of development of the technology, particularly, insufficient techno-economic viability vis-à-vis any competing products. As I mention frequently in the TT Guide, for successful commercialisation, it is simply not enough to have proven the concept at the lab level or even at the industrial level. Very many technologies appear very promising at the lab level but fail or cannot achieve the minimum performance or cost-benefit ratio required once they are tested in industry. For commercialisation to succeed, you need to follow diligently and complete successfully all nine preparatory stages that I discuss in the TT Guide. Most importantly, you have to reach and achieve the 3rd Critical Milestone which is the "techno-economic Viability" criterion (corresponding approximately to TRL 7). If you cannot show conclusively that your new technology can be commercialised viably now or in the future, you should not bother with a start-up – it will surely fail.

A further situation that you might face as a start-up is, ironically, one born of one's own technological success. To put it simply, a new smart-alec "kid on the block" is rarely popular. Competing companies will not take lightly to a competing technology which is so good that it threatens their own market presence. They will use all means in their disposal – many only marginally legal and often not at all fair – to prevent you from entering their markets.

This actually happens often enough to be a serious unfair obstacle to development in many areas. A colleague of mine recently discovered that a simple treatment of a natural inorganic mineral makes a great exfoliating scrub with no side effects and excellent performance. The cost-benefit ratio is excellent, and the market is ripe since this seems to be the only absolutely natural scrub on the market. After extensive testing, he decided that commercialisation could succeed, especially for individuals looking for natural products since many people have become sensitive to many of the unnatural – chemical – ingredients in the many commercial cosmetics. Unfortunately, after he introduced the new product to the market, the result was unexpected and disappointing. Trying to place the product in various stores, he encountered an immediate negative response not from the public but from the large competing manufacturers which directly threatened the stores that they would withdraw all of their products if they – the stores – allowed any such competing materials on their shelves! He is still struggling to find the right distribution channel, but it is an uphill struggle against established vested interests against any novel competing products. This is obviously a most destructive and unfair practice by market competitors that should be illegal but which is incredibly difficult to fight.

There are many other aspects and situations which could potentially present serious risks to the commercialisation of your technology via a start-up or a spin-off company. Although some are extraneous, many are directly related to the challenges of running a company. In Fig. 17.1, I have indicated the most important categories of non-technical risks (fully detailed in the TT Guide), where the size of the balloon indicates the relative importance of the risk type, as indicated by its effect on success at commercialisation.

Unfortunately, in the case of a start-up company which has not yet been set up, in many situations it is not easy or even possible to identify *in advance* the risks you might have to face, let alone find ways to mitigate their consequences. This is why in your Business Plan you are expected to discuss *all potential* risks – i.e. all scenario that could derail your plans – and show how you are prepared to address them if they occur. Risk management as a strategy is actually extremely fruitful in any case as it allows you to consider your venture from the viewpoint of an outsider and, by playing "devil's advocate", identify risk areas which you might not have considered before.

Regarding mitigation actions, a start-up is by definition not in a strong position to face up to market or competitors' threats, and it might thus pay you to consider joining forces with a stronger company in the field as soon as you are ready technologically. In other words, as soon as your start-up is ready to enter the market with a commercial product, you could consider a joint venture with a stronger company – even a competitor – to weather the market resistance from a position

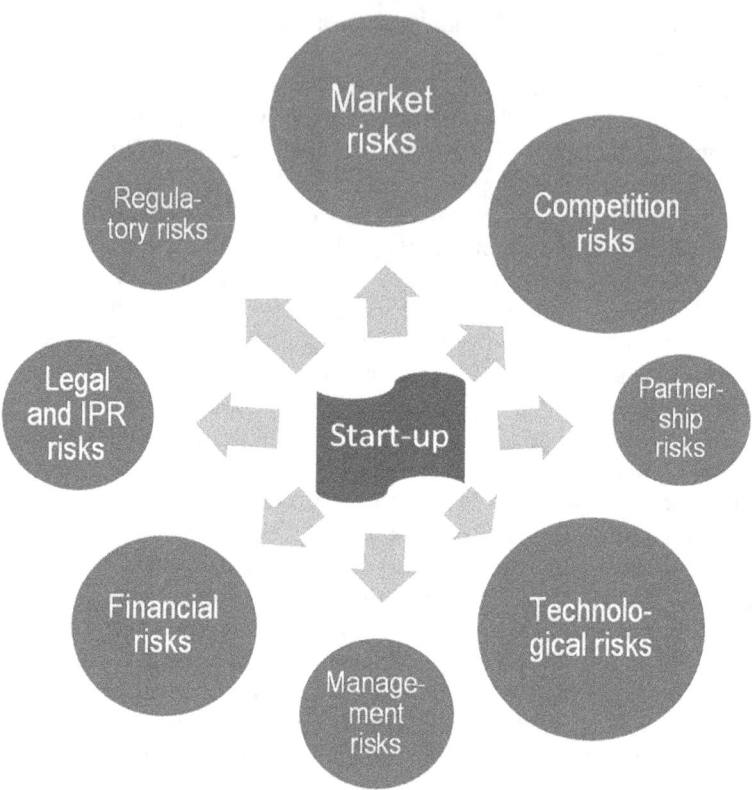

Fig. 17.1 The main categories of risk for technology commercialisation via a start-up company. For more details and SWOT analysis and strategies for analysing, predicting, and handling risk, see the TT Guide

of strength. Such strategic alliances are used by many companies as they offer strong synergies in many respects, especially regarding market presence. For example, if you have developed a new sensor and are now ready for market entry, consider whether a joint venture with a strong sensor manufacturer or system integrator may offer easier and safer market entry than you trying alone.

The important thing to accept (and expect) is that any type of business venture will have risks associated with it. Success is therefore dependent on the degree of mitigation of the most important of these risks and, in general, your own management of their consequences and impact on your business. In the TT Guide, I include a detailed discussion and analysis of a number of risky situations that can occur during commercialisation which can help you to develop your own strategy. All start-ups face challenges, but the ones that succeed are always the ones that were well prepared, especially as regards risk management and mitigation.

In Summary

Running a company involves taking many risks, but starting up a new company involves many more risks, nearly all critical. But you can't win as an entrepreneur unless you are willing to take *well researched, calculated,* and *weighed* risks. This means that since all business ventures have risks associated with them, one of your preparatory activities as an aspiring entrepreneur should include a detailed study of all potential risks, as well as clear identification, as early as possible, of the means and solutions to manage these risks, i.e. the means to minimise them or mitigate them.

18. Protect Your Technology... But Not Too Much!

Intellectual property (IP) protection has always been one of the trickiest aspects to get right when running a new technology-based business. If you protect too weakly, you might encourage copying and not be able to fight any infringements that may occur. On the other hand, if you protect too strongly, you might be wasting your money with little benefit. In fact, with very strong and restrictive protection, you might even be obstructing your own freedom for use and also restricting market take-up of your technology. The optimum, as is often the case, is somewhere in the middle, but each situation is different and there is no hard and fast rule that fits everything.

The value of an innovation depends on many parameters, effective protection being one of the most important. Nearly all funding bodies will insist that you have a good protection strategy in place before they consider backing your venture. The underlying assumption is that effective formal protection – i.e. a patent or equivalent – enhances the potential value of the technology by allowing monopolistic marketing and identifying the owner of the technology (and the production company thereof) while blocking attempts by competing entities at marketing the same technology or restricting the new technology's market presence. It is therefore imperative that your technology is *optimally* protected and safeguarded before any products based on it are offered to the market.

Ideally your protection strategy should be clarified and strengthened even before your technology is out of the lab, but I accept that this is not always possible. For instance, you may not know which are the most promising applications that you should declare in your patent, information which usually influences the functionality and characteristics of a technology. Nevertheless, before you can reach the 2nd Critical Milestone safely (i.e. proven Technological Feasibility, see the TT guide), it is highly recommended to have a good protection strategy in place. Primarily, this means that you should not publish or make known in any way any of the critical underlying principles before you apply for a patent. But even when you do apply for formal protection, it is never a good idea to disclose all of your secrets (the "Core Know-how") in the patent. As I explained in the TT Guide, it is usually perfectly feasible to disclose the general, generic principles in a publication or a patent (you do after all need to advertise your technology) without giving away the key aspects that make your technology competitive. In this way, you are correctly identified as the owner of the technology without giving away its valuable secrets. Of course, only you know which secrets should be protected for this purpose. It could be a tiny amount of a catalyst or another chemical added during processing which would be difficult to discover afterwards or a certain thermal treatment that initiates a crucial change in structure, or a certain timed delay during processing, etc. The general idea is to keep secret any step that cannot be reverse-engineered later by any competing entity. Because you can be sure that, if your technology turns out to be well-performing and competitive, there will be many attempts at trying to work out how to copy it.

This is the key point that makes a protection strategy effective: the capability of advertising the new technology's benefits with reference to underlying principles without the danger of losing your competitive edge. In other words, your protection strategy should guarantee confidentiality and security while ensuring you freedom for use and effective dissemination. This can be quite tricky to arrange, but it is the critical aspect that can assure you success during commercialisation.

The challenge of finding an optimum protection strategy becomes even more pronounced in the case when a piece of valuable know-how is, in retrospect, more or less *obvious* to a skilled person working in this field. As such you cannot get it patented (non-obviousness is one of the three major criteria where many patent applications fail, the other two being absolute novelty and utility), so your best solution is to keep it secret. In fact, a start-up company is a much more effective way to protect such know-how than most other technology-transfer routes since you can set up confidentiality safeguards during production by allowing access to such secret know-how only on a need-to-know basis. This is usually done by organising your production in modules or stages which produce sub-systems which are then integrated together at the final stage by secure staff.

The production of an electro-mechanical sensor I once happened to be involved in is a good example of this. The various sub-systems such as electrical, electronic, mechanical, and various interfaces were produced independently and only integrated together at the final stage just before quality control. In fact, one of the production modules, the machining of the sensor element, had been outsourced so as to reduce even more the possibility of confidentiality leakage. All of this can be arranged in any technology transfer route, but it is much easier with a start-up company.

Let's consider another example, with a twist. A research group in Germany recently developed a new device – a new actuator for controlled delivery of medicines – which is based on a new material system. The key to this system is a quirky physical response to electrical stimuli which they came across by accident and which, in retrospect, would not be surprising (i.e. more or less obvious) to an expert scientist in this field. This type of fortuitous discovery happens often in laboratories, sometimes as a side effect of some material process or treatment and other times as a result of a (serendipitous) test that was applied wrongly. While their invention offers better performance and easier usage than competing technologies, it is difficult to protect since the key element (the physical response) is not patentable. What can they do to ensure that they get some benefit from it while keeping it free for commercialisation? They can protect it of course, up to a point (see the TT Guide for more secrets of effective protection), but it would be difficult to avoid having it copied if they license it out. If they license it out, they will have to disclose everything to the producer and hope for the best. With a tight-enough contract (with strict confidentiality clauses), they could be alright, as long as they have access rights to all production and accounting activities. The risk would still be substantial. In this case, I believe the best way for this research group to proceed would be to set up a start-up (or spin-off) company within which they will need to find a way to produce the actuator while ensuring that the underlying principle is embedded in one of the sub-systems and obscured by other sub-systems. This approach helps to confuse reverse-engineering analysis, although it does not eliminate the likelihood of it happening completely.

Effective protection of your technology will also help you get through the pilot and industrial tests securely, but your protection strategy should be monitored and strengthened on a continuous basis. For example, while the original patent covers the generic aspects of your invention and you have listed a number of potential applications, you should be on the lookout for any new fields of application that it may be useful for and patent it for them too. One of my own sensors was originally developed for space but it has since been adapted for terrestrial industrial use. By the way, I never patented it as the underlying principle is known, but the application method is nicely obscured.

As mentioned above, formal protection of your technology while keeping key aspects secret offers the added benefit of freedom for further development and use. This means it is an effective way of guaranteeing that no one else will patent it to try to restrict it in order to protect their own products or technologies. This means that even if you can't afford the expense of patenting your technology world-widely, by submitting an application within your own country you are effectively declaring ownership at the date of disclosure and thereby preventing anyone else from trying to patent it and restricting your own use. Of course, you get the same result and even more securely by publishing it in a relatively obscure journal.

Finally, when considering the various options open to you for protection, it is worth considering the benefits of a strategy of open disclosure of the generic aspects of a new technology, for example in a publication, accompanied by formal protection of only certain optimum manifestations of the technology in the form of devices or products for specific applications. By following such a strategy, you benefit from exposure while increasing dissemination of the advantages of the new technology.

Effective protection of assets, especially non-tangible assets such as know-how, is critical for the success of your new enterprise. Entrepreneurial success often depends on how carefully you have prepared and maintained your protection strategy.

In Summary

Effective protection of your core technology and know-how is critical for the success of your enterprise. If you protect too weakly, you might encourage copying and not be able to fight any infringements that may occur. If you protect too strongly, you might be wasting your money with little benefit. In fact, with very strong and restrictive protection, you might even be obstructing your own freedom for use and also restricting market take-up of your technology.

Viability, Not Just Feasibility   19

As scientific and technological researchers, our main aim is the development of novel or improved technologies (materials, processes, devices, systems, software, etc.) with enhanced applicability in society. As we get on with our business of identifying new phenomena and improving our understanding, we focus our technical efforts on developing technologies that are stronger, faster, denser, tougher, more precise, more resistant, and so on – i.e. better than what is already being used for a particular application. In other words, we emphasise technical competitiveness with minor regard to the potential applicability of our technology.

This "isolation in our lab" is actually necessary since, in general, a novel technological invention is judged first on its technological merits and characteristics without particular regard to its eventual application. We need to keep our options open after all. Only after the proof of concept (first Critical Milestone) is achieved can we then start looking towards potential applicability and, after suitable protection, reach the second Critical Milestone at which point in time we should have proven the Technical Feasibility of our technology for the targeted applications.

However, proving the technical feasibility of a technology is only the beginning as far as the market is concerned. As soon as we leave the lab and start pilot and industrial testing (probably during the transfer of the technology to your new start-up), the whole emphasis of our RD must change. At this point, we must accept that no matter how good a technology is (or promises to be), it is its applicability and especially its "viability" for a particular application that matter most. *Viability*, then, is the capability of our technology to be accepted for a particular application at a particular time. And this is unfortunately a very slippery concept which depends on many parameters – most of which are independent of our ability to influence them – but also the technical capability of our technology. It is, however, a crucial aspect that you need to address and analyse convincingly in your Business Plan. You need to consider the potential markets and offer convincing viable solutions for each of them, including the effects of various scenario. Only when the balance is positive (i.e. there is a prospect for substantial return on investment within a reasonable time period) should you consider setting up an enterprise for commercialisation.

Viability of a technology means different things to different users, but the fundamental proviso is that it must take into account the financial and societal constraints of the application it is aimed at. In other words, the market will ask, "Can this new technology deliver superior performance, safely and at the right price for this application at this time?" This is where the difficulty arises, since the last four parameters – safety, price, application, and timing – are interdependent and usually dependent on extraneous factors that you have little or no control over.

There are many parameters, including the above, that affect the viability of a technology in a particular market or application:

- Cost of the new technology vis-à-vis competing technologies
- Cost-benefit ratio
- Previous experience and perception of the market (positive or negative)
- Skill level of potential users
- Relative ease of production and use
- Safety of production and use
- Existence of enabling technologies (e.g. materials, processes, etc.)
- Constraints of regulations

And that's not all. The viability of a technology at the time of expected commercialisation is also dependent on parameters such as the current position of the investment cycle of the user (has the original investment on the existing technology of the potential users been repaid yet?), general state of the economy, any current trends (materials, design, etc.), and others.

So how can you estimate the actual viability of your technology and go about enhancing it? This sounds like a tall order but in fact the solution could be more or less in your hands, early on. You should ensure right at the outset (i.e. before you take it out of the lab) that your new technology can be made safely and is adaptable and flexible in its construction and applicability. If you can achieve this, you can ensure that you can address many different applications at different price and quality levels. If this is not possible, viability may prove to be elusive.

Let's consider some examples to clarify these points. In a previous chapter, I mentioned an electro-mechanical sensor for measuring in situ the depth of wear of protective layers when direct access to them is impossible. The original impetus for designing it was to monitor the depth of recession (i.e. wear) of the heat shield of space capsules as they hurtle at high speeds through the atmosphere. This is still the main application (techno-economic viability is optimised), but the same sensor has now been adapted (by simplifying construction, reducing dimensional constraints, and reducing overall cost) for use in industrial boilers, furnaces, etc. and is being commercialised via a spin-off company. In fact, we have projected that income from terrestrial industrial applications will be much higher in the future because of the much larger market size. It is clear that the viability of the sensor for industrial applications could only be ensured by lowering the overall cost substantially. Unfortunately, the economic downturn and the covid19 pandemic slowed us down considerably, but efforts are still on-going.

A further example, from the medical field this time, introduces the aspect of safety in the estimation of viability. A few years ago, I discussed with a senior RD manager of a multinational pharmaceutical the prospects for a nanotechnology-based medicine for a particular ailment which is widespread globally. This was a major project for their company since the existing medicinal preparations were losing their efficacy and the patents were running out. An RD project had proven the feasibility of the new technological approach, and the first clinical trials were already being planned since the detailed techno-economic analyses indicated strongly that the viability of the technology was strong. However, at the same period, the first questions were raised regarding the suitability of using standard safety protocols to determine the safety of nanomedicines, since it had just been reported in independent studies that generic side effects of nanomedicines included some that had never been observed before, including mitochondrial damage. This led to the decision to delay all trials until the situation could be clarified. A large series of studies has since been launched in Europe to clarify this question and draw up new guidelines. Although this has been welcomed by all, it means that the viability of new nanomedicines cannot be estimated yet. Most clinical trials have had to be stopped and many projects postponed. The jury is still out on the safety of nanomedicine (some studies are still proceeding, 10 years later), but this has meant that many projects have been dropped or delayed due to unknowable viability.

A final example, from the field of energy production, introduces the aspect of a "reasonable return on investment" in the calculation of viability. As intimated above, the calculation of viability should include the question, "Is the technology able to generate enough income over a reasonable period to cover the total investment for its development?" This is actually one of the main questions that you are required to address when you prepare the business plan for your enterprise, and it relates to the willingness (or need or demand) of the market to pay enough for it over a long enough period to get back at least as much as you invested in the project.

The current push towards a reduction of the dependence of energy generation on fossil fuels has brought back into the limelight a number of technologies that had been considered non-viable in the past. One of these is geothermy: the exploitation of the naturally constant temperature that exists underground for heating (or cooling) offices and houses. The problem with this technology has always been the high capital cost involved in digging the holes and then installing the pipes, storage tanks, controls, and interfaces within the existing systems. In volcanic countries like Iceland, this is no problem as they have huge thermal capacity just a few tens of metres underground, but it is more difficult in other places. Interestingly, hot countries like my own (Greece) can benefit by the constant *much lower* temperature existing underground, even at the height of summer. But even so, viability is not always guaranteed. Recently, I have witnessed the installation of such a system (for a total office and lab area of approximately 600 m^2) at a cost of about 200k Euros. Considering the underground temperature is approximately constant and an average use of heating over about 3 months of winter and cooling over about 4 months of summer and moderate insulation efficiency, I estimated that the return on investment will take more than 15 years to be realised. This is obviously too long and I cannot consider this technology viable.

The bottom line, therefore, can be put quite simply: do not consider commercialisation unless the viability of your technology – measured by all means such as cost-benefit, safety, adaptability, applicability, and so on – is clearly such that there is a significant chance that the investment will be at least matched by income over the first few years of your company's operations.

In Summary

No matter how good a technology is (or promises to be), it is its applicability and especially its "viability" for a particular application that matter most. *Viability*, then, can be defined as the capability of the technology to be accepted for a particular application at a particular time. This involves mainly techno-economic competitiveness (i.e. cost-benefit ratio) but other aspects as well, such as perception, acceptability, compatibility, etc.

Skilling and Re-skilling 20

Business enterprises are based on human capital. Whether any enterprise sinks or swims depends directly on the knowledge and skills of its workers. You, as the inventor-researcher, offer the vision and the scientific and technological foundations, but the day-to-day operations in the company will be carried out by skilled workers, each offering their expertise in their specific area. And, more often than not, it is the lack of properly skilled workers that is responsible for the failure of a company, especially in a technologically shifting business environment. A company which does not recognise ahead of time the need for skilling and re-skilling of its workers will find itself in trouble sooner or later.

Finding the right persons for each job in a company can be a huge challenge, especially for a new start-up which is aiming to develop and produce a completely new technology for which the specific skills are, by definition, non-existent or at least not well-known. Again, it is in your hands, as you are the only person with the specific technological knowledge needed to further develop and commercialise the new technology and to develop the skills of the workers in the company. If you are lucky enough to be joined in the new company by a graduate student or another worker from your laboratory, then their specialist skills will form the knowledge core upon which you will depend for support in training new workers. If you are not so lucky, everything will depend on you.

Acquiring the skills to carry out a specific task in a technology-based business is far more difficult and time-consuming than ordinary training. Skilling means becoming an expert in a specific job, one that the company can depend on. A trained operator of a machine is able to operate the machine satisfactorily, but a *skilled* operator of the machine is able to understand the workings and quirks of the machine and fix problems when they arise so that production can continue unhindered. A skilled person is one who has undergone full training *and* acquired extensive experience in the (particular) job and task at hand.

Young workers straight out of university require completely different training than experienced staff coming from another job, even in a similar industry. A young graduate has acquired a basic understanding of the field, perhaps with some exposure to the specific technology of your start-up, but needs extensive on-the-job training and a few years of experience before he or she is skilled enough to take on a responsible job. The advantage of this however is that these young workers are less likely to be influenced (or constrained) by prior experience, and so, theoretically at least, their training can be focused on the new technology from the get-go.

In contrast, an experienced worker coming from a similar job in another company may already have the general training to carry out the job (saving you training time and effort), but they may also bring with them certain prejudices and preconceptions arising from their way of working in their previous employment. Depending on the type of task they are expected to do, such preconceptions may be problematic since new technologies generally need new approaches and new methods. Re-skilling of such experienced workers can be a time-consuming job in its own right since they first have to forget their previous experience and then learn the ropes of the new job.

New enterprises in new technological fields – e.g. nanotechnology or artificial intelligence (AI) – encounter quite severe problems in finding specialist skilled staff. Even experienced workers in similar fields may not be very useful directly and may require extensive additional re-skilling to be able to deal with the specialist tasks needed. Graduate students who have worked in your lab on the technologies needed are generally a better bet in this case. I recall a situation where a large project developing a new nanostructured powdered material was seriously delayed because the – otherwise highly experienced – staff at the materials manufacturing partner implementing the new technology could not get their heads around the different production techniques needed and kept on producing wrong powders. Most of the re-skilling there had to be carried out by the original laboratory workers who took on the task of training the industrial workers, which reduced production speed. It took many months to get things working satisfactorily.

In another example, skilled workers accustomed to a particular chemical process for activating an ore at a mining plant found it difficult to learn to use a much faster activation process that was based on a combination of the same chemical process (using a much lower volume of the same chemical) and a microwave-based thermal treatment. Because the microwave treatment was opaque to them, they continued using the same amount of chemicals, thereby inadvertently cancelling out the advantages of the microwave treatment. Re-skilling in this case proved quite difficult and time-consuming, and eventually, the company gives up on the microwave assist component of the process at a considerable cost.

The training and re-skilling needs of company staff need to be considered right at the outset and even analysed in the business plan for your new enterprise. In this regard, the location of the new company also needs to be taken into account since the financial benefits of setting up the company in an area of lower skills level may be cancelled out by the increased expenses of finding and skilling or re-skilling critical personnel. The actual or perceived difficulty of finding skilled personnel can also become a factor in the decision to finance a company. In a case I know from about 15 years ago a business plan for a new venture by an existing manufacturing company in the ceramics field in South East Europe to produce electro-ceramics was considered too risky by a venture capital firm due to the fact that the location of the new venture could not guarantee an adequate skills level on the part of local personnel. Even taking into account the very high tax discounts offered by the government of that country, the cost of attracting, re-skilling, and keeping expert personnel was judged too high.

Specialist skilling – and the lack thereof – is considered so important by large companies that many subsidise university departments to set up highly specialist courses and laboratories where students can be trained early on in the new technologies. Some of these students join those companies after graduation more or less ready skilled and can take on the job of passing on their skills to other personnel. Such proactive actions are ubiquitous in the USA, China, and lately India and the European Union in advanced technology fields such as nanotechnology, microelectronics, business and AI coding, advanced medical technologies, and others.

While your new start-up will not be able to subsidise a university or compete with such companies, you should plan how to ensure the availability of young graduates from such departments for your company. If your enterprise is particularly dependent on skilled graduates, you should consider locating in areas where they could be attracted. In fact, the availability of specialist and highly skilled personnel acts as a magnet for other similarly interested young persons asking to be trained, eventually creating pools of highly skilled workers. This is one of the reasons why the famous Silicon Valley has attracted such a high density of skilled personnel. Similar hubs now exist in various regions globally such as Cambridge in the UK, Lausanne in Switzerland, Grenoble in France, Mumbai and elsewhere in India, Tokyo in Japan, and a few regions in China and Taiwan.

Training, skilling, and re-skilling of personnel are critical activities and important assets for all successful technology-based companies. While the cost is often high – personnel may be expected to attend re-skilling sessions regularly to keep up with technological developments and they may demand high salaries – the returns are even higher. The capacity of attracting and keeping skilled, specialist personnel is one of the main pillars of any new successful technology-driven enterprise.

In Summary

Day-to-day operations in a company are carried out by skilled workers, each offering their expertise in their specific area. And, more often than not, it is the lack of properly skilled workers that is responsible for the failure of a company, especially in a technologically shifting business environment. A company which does not recognise ahead of time the need for skilling and re-skilling of its workers will find itself in trouble sooner or later.

The Market Is Your Guide 21

Nearly all of the technological research we carry out is more or less aimed at some future application. Even what is called "basic research" is nothing more than upstream research that could one day be adapted for a future application. By "application" we mean that the results of the research could find some use by society (people, institutions, companies, etc.), in some field or sector. This is what is loosely called "the market", and it should be your main guide in your attempt to commercialise your invention. It is the market that guides and dictates whether a new invention has potential value and might therefore be turned into an innovative product or service one day.

The market, as defined above, is fluid. Trends, fads, industrial practices, societal sensitivities, personal aspirations, institutional directions, cost constraints, state regulations, standards, and guidelines can all change and the market changes with them. As discussed previously, it is crucial that you "listen" to the market, keep a watch on market developments, and always be ready to make necessary changes in order to follow and – if you are influential enough – lead the market in your field and sector.

But, as I mentioned many times, be very careful to distinguish between what you'd *like* to develop – your pet projects – and what the market really *expects* or *needs*. For this, you need to keep in close contact with both producers and users and make sure your technologies address the real needs – and constraints – of the market. Health restrictions on many materials, for example, mean that an otherwise excellent device cannot be applied for a medical condition because it contains small amounts of banned materials such as nickel or lead or certain polymers, considered toxic. Such restrictions are becoming more and more widespread so you have to keep your eyes peeled as new materials are added all the time. [1] In the field of industrial pigments – used to colour textiles, plastics, ceramics, paper, paints, inks, and many other applications – a cheap stable red pigment has become a holy grail because the

---

[1] For example in the European Union, the REACH regulation controls all materials used or sold.

brightest red pigments available used lead and cadmium oxides which have now been restricted. Many similar challenges exist and efforts are under way globally to substitute materials used in many applications, even ones that have been around for years. Even some stainless steels are being questioned for their use as high temperature cooking utensils because of their nickel content, although it is at present difficult to see what could provide a suitable replacement for them. Such challenges of course are excellent opportunities for the development of new technologies.

Sometimes the market shifts just as you are in the process of developing a technology to answer a need that was evident but then became obsolete. For example, high-density BluRay™ disks were developed just as high-density flash memories (solid-state read-write memories) and associated mobile music players (mp3 and so on) came onto the market. Only one of these technologies could win the race for the market's favour and BluRays disappeared.

The last 60 or so years have seen more changes in the way the world operates, connects, and communicates than in its whole preceding history. And of these changes, the last 30 years, with the emergence of personal computers, mobile communication, and above all the Internet, have been nothing less than earth-shaking. Cutting-edge technologies that were lauded as critical technologies during the twentieth century have now all but disappeared in many countries, superseded by today's even more remarkable counterparts. For example, the fax, the landline telephone, the electric typewriter, calculators, and dot-matrix printers, to name but a few, have now all recently become almost-extinct relics. In their place, we have email, mobile telephony, laser printers, smart phones, electronic pads, and so on. Even the desktop personal computer that used to be ubiquitous everywhere has almost completely given way to laptops, tablets, net-books, and smartphones. The 3D printer is fast becoming the tool of choice for prototyping and for producing unique and intricate products with internal surfaces that cannot be produced in any other way. People are "meeting" more than ever before in virtual meeting places by live teleconferencing and are freely and excitedly exchanging views and opinions in the various social media outlets that populate the Internet. In fact, these technologies were instrumental in enabling the world to function more or less normally during the global covid19 emergency.

These changes have all one thing in common: they were all made possible by society – and the market – pushing and expecting better, faster, more convenient, and stronger technologies for business but also for everyday life. It is always the market that guides the research that makes these changes possible.

Sometimes the market is "unreasonable" in its expectations or demands, but research nevertheless tries hard to provide solutions, not always satisfactory or successful. For example, the age-old dream of humans to be able to "fly" at will has always spurred a large number of designs and attempts, nearly all unsuccessful and many deadly. Be that as it may, in the last few years it seems that we are eventually getting a little closer to this dream with new types of jet-packs (marginally improved) or the very dangerous looking rocket-propelled suits designed and flown by Yves Rossy, a daredevil Swiss military-trained pilot. In any case of course, such endeavours have always been accompanied and supported by technologies in propulsion, navigation, aerodynamics, etc. These are important long-lasting successes that eventually spill over in other applications and systems.

Another interesting area in which the market – supported by regulations – has been instrumental in enabling major changes is personal transport where the desire for cars with lower need for liquid fuels has spurred the development of hydrogen-fuelled engines, hybrid and electric power trains, and more exotic ideas such as compressed air and water-based engines. All of these have been the motivation and impetus for many side developments in areas such hydrogen production and storage, new motors and storage batteries, energy-harvesting from braking, flexible solar panels, new energy-distribution systems, and many others. The same incentives – supported and, alternatively, coerced by environmental regulations – have also given rise to the development of many types of sensors for emission control, fuel consumption, catalyst temperature optimisation, internal heating control, anti-lock braking systems, anti-skid systems, and even micro-radars as parking aids. The latest efforts have seen the development of self-driving cars, parking assist, collision warning and avoidance, and more. In all of these cases, the public, i.e. the market, has either been asking for these developments or the production companies have tried to pre-empt them based on the expectation that people will be attracted to them once their applicability for everyday life is proven.

The food sector has been awash with new technologies driven by market expectations and demands for fresh convenience foods as well as healthier alternatives to existing choices. At the same time, stricter health and safety regulations have meant that many new technologies in packaging (and materials for them), food storage, and food distribution have appeared. High-tech nanotechnologies are under development with the aim of detecting contamination during food processing as well as at the point of sale, warning producers and consumers by using coloured indicators and so on.

With the eye towards reduction of environmental impact, many packaging materials manufacturers have also turned their attention to new and bio-based materials. With new stricter legislation, the European Union is leading the way in banning the use of single-use plastics and insisting that all packaging must be recyclable or biodegradable and must contain a good fraction of recycled materials. This has spurred fresh research on new paper or plastic-based packaging materials based on corn, cereals, potatoes, and even agricultural waste. Unfortunately, this has impacted food prices, so the emphasis is now shifting to low grade foods or waste.

When it comes to the two-way feedback between the market and society and RD, the medical field plays a large role. A large number of technological developments have appeared during the last decades which have all but revolutionised surgery (surgical microscopes, remote, robotic surgery, live scans and technologies in blood control, infection detectors, etc.), in vivo diagnostic sensors (continuous blood monitors for sugar level and insulin, continuous monitoring of various blood and plasma factors and indicators, etc.), in vivo medicinal drug delivery systems for insulin and many other medicines (skin patches, embedded micro-systems, etc.), and in numerous other areas. New materials and devices have also been developed which promise new and more efficient artificial hearts, bladders, skin, and even kidneys and livers. New technologies have also been developed to satisfy the need for treating athletic injuries such as artificial spinal disks, knee caps, bones, ligaments, and skin – the list goes on and on.

In practice, therefore, it is in your hands to make sure that your RD is focused toward a potential application in society and the market. You should proactively maintain a regular market watch by visiting industrial fairs and exhibitions, regularly perusing market literature, as well as publishing short technology briefs in industrial journals.

As stated at the beginning of this chapter, if you are to succeed in your commercialisation drive, it is the market that should guide your RD and industrial adaptation efforts, especially if you are operating a start-up. You should design your technology based on what the market needs, not what you would like to do.

In Summary

Even results from "basic research" projects may 1 day be adapted for future applications which means that those results could find some use by society (people, institutions, companies, etc.), in some field or sector. This is what is loosely called "the market", and it should be your main guide in your attempt to commercialise your invention. It is the market – with all its slipperiness and transience – that guides and dictates us whether a new invention has potential value and might therefore be turned into an innovative product or service 1 day.

Position, Position, Position 22

There is an old adage that says that there are three criteria for choosing a house: location, location, and location. In other words, no matter what the quality of the house, it is its geographic location (position) that really decides its innate market worth. Unfortunately, as trends come and go, valuable locations do not always remain so, but that's another matter entirely.

The same holds true for enterprises, with one important difference. It is not the geographic position that gives value to an enterprise, but its *market positioning*. This is a bit of a slippery concept that is worth dwelling on as it is often the deciding factor in determining whether an enterprise will succeed or fail.

To begin with, market positioning is not the same as "market position", which usually denotes the relative sales volume achieved by the enterprise in a specific market with respect to its competitors in that market. In fact, the way "market positioning" is used in this book differs a little from the usual definition. "Market positioning" is often defined as, for example, "An effort to influence consumer perception of a brand or product relative to the perception of competing brands or products. Its objective is to occupy a clear, unique, and advantageous position in the consumer's mind". [1]

In this book, I use "market positioning" in a more literal sense to indicate a multidimensional activity where your enterprise needs to identify where its technology fits in each dimension and then develop a market strategy based on your findings. Each dimension refers to a different theme which generally has two (but could have more) opposite poles between which will be the correct position for your technology. In all cases, the correct market position will reflect the characteristics both of your technology and your business vision. Ideally, you should aim to get all of these position dimensions correct right from the word go, although corrections are possible later. Bear in mind that your market positioning may be different for each of your technology manifestations. For example, your technology may be adapted both

---

[1] BusinessDictionary.com (2016).

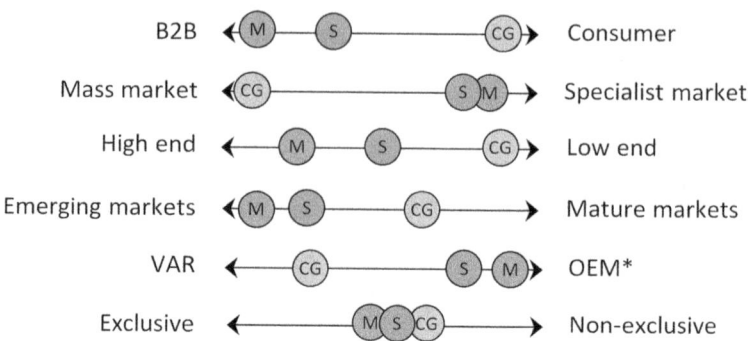

Fig. 22.1 Six market positioning dimensions with illustrative examples for three generic technologies: M, advanced material; CG, computer game; S, sensor; VAR, value-added reseller; OEM, original equipment manufacturer

for space and for terrestrial applications, each of which would then have different market positioning.

Market positioning could be taken into account even during the early research stages so that RD is planned and executed accordingly. Many technologies are mainly (or only) applicable industrially and are not meant to be available directly to end users. In other words, they have to be commercialised as a business-to-business (B2B) concept where you supply other businesses for them to incorporate your technology into their products or services. These are the technologies that consumer and other products are built out of and built with. In fact, these B2B technologies are the majority under development in research centres and universities. New materials and processes, new methods, protocols, industrial software, most types of sensors and actuators and other embeddable devices, motors and engines, electronic transistors, chips, circuits, etc., all fall under this category. If your technology is a B2B technology, then your enterprise will be dealing almost exclusively with other manufacturers, and naturally, your marketing strategy has to take this into account. A B2B market position means that you will publish articles and advertise in trade journals, attend trade and business fairs and exhibitions, and so on.

On the other hand, if your technology is closer to the end user market – for example, if you are aiming to develop and supply ready products or services – your market position is closer to the consumer and your marketing will be based on direct advertising in mass media, consumer journals, etc. We'll have more to say about the B2B vs. direct-to-consumer dimension below.

As an aid for visualisation, Fig. 22.1 shows the main market positioning dimensions applicable for technologies and associated products. It is not an exhaustive listing as other positioning dimensions may exist depending on the nature of your technology and your own growth strategy may dictate specialised dimensions in specific markets as well. Three examples of products and technologies have been placed on the various dimensions on the diagram for illustration, and these are discussed below: an advanced material, a computer game, and a sensor. Keep in mind that within each of these market positioning dimensions, you may also have secondary ranges referring to application sectors, fields, etc. which can aid your detailed strategy planning. Here I'm only discussing the basic level positioning.

Let us look at the dimensions in Fig. 22.1 in detail. The first dimension ("B2B ⟵⟶ Consumer"), as discussed above, refers to whether your technology is destined for incorporation into an instrument, machine, process, etc. that is made by your or another enterprise or whether it can be offered directly to consumers in the market. As mentioned above, most technologies usually under development in public research laboratories are aimed at industrial use (i.e. they are positioned close to the B2B side of the dimension), whereas industrial laboratories generally aim at developing actual products (or processes, etc.) to be made available directly to consumers. In keeping with this understanding, then, a new advanced material (M in Fig. 22.1) would naturally be aimed at being incorporated into another technology (device, machine, etc.), whereas a computer game (CG) would be aimed directly at consumers. A sensor (S), however, is mainly aimed at being embedded in an instrument, but it may also be sold directly to consumers. Positioning in this particular dimension is generally easy to decide although it is possible that over time, technologies may shift. For example, whereas simulation software (using e.g. Finite Element Methods) was developed (and is still mainly used) as an aid in mechanical designing, it has become so user-friendly that it can easily be aimed at (specialist) consumers too.

The second market positioning dimension listed in Fig. 22.1 refers to whether your technology is aimed at the mass market or specialist (niche) markets. This may not sound relevant for B2B technologies, but you will want to decide whether to focus your RD efforts towards a mass-market collaborator or a specialist market. While a computer game, then, should clearly be aimed at a mass market, new materials and sensors are generally going to be deployed in niche areas.

The next dimension is particularly important since it is directly linked with the cost of manufacturing. While a new material may be manufactured to precise specifications at high cost (placing it close to the high-end side), it may also be produced under less stringent controls and therefore cost less. In the latter case, it would usually be aimed at less demanding applications. A sensor may also be placed on either side of the spectrum by adjusting, for instance, its resolution and capabilities. Finally, a mass-market consumer game will generally be aimed at the low end of the spectrum (irrespective of whether it is produced to very high specifications) to try to win a greater fraction of the market.

The fourth dimension included in Fig. 22.1 brings in an evolutionary aspect to market positioning and asks you to consider whether your technology has become relevant due to the emergence of a new market (e.g. renewable energy generation, new medical treatments, environmental protection) or whether it should be aimed at mature markets, perhaps in the hope of replacing existing technologies. In this regard, many new materials and sensors are being developed as a response to new, emerging markets and situations (environmental protection, climate emergency, etc.), but a computer game is mainly aimed at a mature market. However, these are not exclusive positionings, since new materials, new sensors, and so on may be able to replace existing ones in mature markets.

The next dimension listed comprises a special case of the B2B vs. consumer dimension. It asks whether you will be aiming your technology at the actual producers of branded equipment ("original equipment manufacturer" or OEM) or to intermediate consumers ("value-added resellers" or VAR) who will buy your product, rebrand it, and sell it as their own. This happens frequently nowadays and helps manufacturers to increase their income by leveraging the market share of branded VARs to their mutual benefit. Generally, any technology such as a new material, device, or sensor can be positioned at any point on the scale, but a ready product (e.g. a computer game) will probably be closer to the OEM edge.

Finally, the last dimension considered in Fig. 22.1 refers to your business strategy with regard to licensing of your technology. In the TT Guide, I have discussed this in detail, but the gist is that an early decision could be made to aim your technology exclusively toward a particular application (or even a particular enterprise) on the basis of a cost-sharing or joint venture RD agreement. Although such a move may exclude other markets and other potential collaborators, it may be necessary as a result of the need for financial and other support. Costly and complicated technologies fall into this category as well as highly specialised ones where there are limited potential users, e.g. technologies specially developed for the space exploration market. The space capsule heat shield sensor successfully developed and produced in my lab falls under this category since there is a very limited niche market.

Market positioning along the above (and perhaps other) dimensions will probably be one of the most important decisions you will have to make as an entrepreneur. The earlier you make it, the easier you will find your market entry later. Although much of the necessary information will probably not be available during the early stages of your research, it is still necessary to keep your mind focused on the various possibilities and choices.

In Summary

The value of a technology (a product or a service, etc.) is mostly dictated by its *market positioning* which is often the deciding factor in determining whether an enterprise will succeed or fail. Correct positioning has many dimensions, but six of them are most critical: high end/low end, B2B or consumer, mass market or niche markets, emerging or mature markets, exclusive or non-exclusive, and value-added reseller or original equipment manufacturer.

Commercialisation Readiness Index 23

Every culture has a saying or proverb equivalent to "more haste, less speed". In other words, if you rush into any business (or, for that matter, any kind of venture) with little preparation and with little regard for the need to "watch your step", you are certain to encounter obstacles in your way that will delay you. On the other hand, it is crucial to be the first to reach the market with your new product and carve your niche before others try to copy you. This is a very real dilemma and quite a difficult balancing act.

The same holds true for your preparations to set up a start-up to commercialise your research results. If, in your enthusiasm to bring your new technology to the market, you do not do your homework diligently and accurately before you embark, you will encounter a myriad delays and even obstacles. Planning is everything: a detailed business plan is essential and the precise execution of your business plan will be critical to your success. Your roots should be strong and secure before you can sprout leaves and fruit! This takes time and effort and you need to find solutions to all eventualities. By considering all possible scenario (especially negative scenario, i.e. risk analysis) and working out solutions, you will be ready for them if they arise.

On the other hand, markets ripe for your technology will not wait. They may be ready for your technology one moment and indifferent the next. Markets nowadays shift and change quickly and what looked like a great opportunity can evaporate quickly, allowing something else to take its place. Even industrial investment cycles are much shorter than they used to be, so the windows of B2B opportunities are generally narrower. In today's fast-paced and changeable markets, a few months or a year is often all you have to demonstrate and prove the worth of your technology. This is particularly evident in mass market products such as computer games, smartphones (and their functionality), foods, cosmetics, clothing, gadgets, clothes, and so on.

You therefore need to strike a balance between the time you take for your preparations, risk analysis, and negotiations and the launch of your new start-up and your products in the market. There are no hard and fast rules for resolving such a dilemma. That said, once you reach Technology Readiness Level 8 (TRL 8, see TT Guide), you are probably at least *technologically* ready to start the speed-up your activities in your start-up company and launch your product or service in the market. So, how would you estimate if you are ready for market launching in all respects?

Commercialisation Readiness Index

To see if you are ready to launch your product in the market, I have prepared a simple system to measure your "*Commercialisation Readiness Index*" or CRI, an index analogous to the TRL. It is calculated by evaluating your readiness for commercialisation against ten criteria, as shown in the scoring matrix in Table 23.1. All these criteria reflect the most important conditions discussed in the previous chapters and which need to be fulfilled before you seriously can consider

Table 23.1 A scoring matrix to determine your aggregate Commercialisation Readiness Index (CRI) (scores shown refer to a real case)

#	Question	Score (tick one box)					
		−3	−2	−1	1	2	3
1	Is the viability of your technology fully proven under market (or industrial) conditions (i.e. is it at TRL 8)?			✓			
2	Have you carried out a detailed risk analysis and worked out solutions and fall-back positions for all major commercialisation risks identified?					✓	
3	Have you carried out an in-depth core market study with regard to its readiness to accept your technology?		✓				
4	Have you identified alternative potential markets that you could target as a fall-back position or at a later stage?					✓	
5	Is your core team ready and committed to the success of the venture?						✓
6	Have you identified various scenario for market entry and worked out a market strategy for each of them?						✓
7	Have you secured enough funds to carry you over the initial period until break-even?				✓		
8	Have you secured critical collaborations with scientific and technological supporting teams?					✓	
9	Have you identified the core suppliers for your raw materials, critical machinery, etc.?				✓		
10	Have you identified marketing routes and distribution channels for your product or technology?				✓		
	Number of ticks in each column (N)	0	1	1	3	3	2
	Weighted totals of each column (N × column score)	0	−2	−1	3	6	6
	Commercialisation Readiness Index (sum of weighted totals/number of questions): CRI				1.2		

commercialising your technology. It is a foregone conclusion that attempting to set up a company or otherwise commercialise a technology that has not reached satisfactory level in any of these criteria is probably a waste of time, or at least will have a lower chance of success.

Let's now see how CRI can be determined and what your steps should be taken afterwards.

Firstly, consider the criteria/questions in Table 23.1 and try to answer them as honestly and objectively as possible regarding your technology. This will give you a good indication of your readiness to launch. Answer all the questions, giving yourself a 3 if the answer is "Of course!" and –3 if your answer is "Hmm, not really". In answering the questions, try to be strict with yourself and do not settle for a neutral answer (that's why I have not included a middle grade). At the end, add up the number of ticks in each column and multiply by the column weight (shown at the top of each column. Finally, add up all the totals and divide by 10 (the number of questions) to obtain your "Commercialisation Readiness Index" (CRI). I have done this and entered replies for a real case I encountered some years ago (an attempt at producing an improved consumer item) which showed that it was not ready for commercialisation yet, especially regarding some of the criteria.

So, what does the overall CRI score tell you? It's simple really. Ultimately, all your answers should be either +2 or +3, but if they are not, then you need to do more work. More specifically:

- If your CRI is negative, don't even think of launching your start-up yet but go back to the drawing board to continue preparations.
- If your result is positive and greater than 1 and you have no ticks in the negative columns, you are moving ahead nicely, but you still have a lot of work in front of you. This is the result we see here (CRI = 1.2) for the attempt at producing an "improved consumer item".
- If your result is more than 2 and you have no negatives, you are on your way, only a little ground still to cover.
- If your CRI is over 2.5 and you have no negative scores, what are you waiting for? The market will not wait long!

All of the questions in Tables 23.1 and 23.2 are critical to the success of your start-up which is why if you score "–3", "–2", or "–1" even in one, then it means that you are not ready to commercialise or leave the laboratory yet. Your main task therefore is to convert these negatives to positives with the central aim being to reach scores of "3" in every question, if possible. A bit of a tall order actually, but not impossible at all.

Continuing with the same real case, the researcher agreed that the CRI was probably too low and went back to the lab and continued working in order to improve her score in questions 1 and 3. She also tried to improve the score for questions 4, 7, and 9 where she initially had scored "1". After about 6 months, we discussed the new situation, and the new scores she estimated are shown in Table 23.2.

Table 23.2 The CRI matrix of the case study in Table 23.1 after improvements in design and prototype production ideas

#	Question	Score (tick one box)					
		−3	−2	−1	1	2	3
1	Is the viability of your technology fully proven under market (or industrial) conditions (i.e. is it at TRL 8)?					✓	
2	Have you carried out a detailed risk analysis and worked out solutions and fall-back positions for all major commercialisation risks identified?					✓	
3	Have you carried out an in-depth core market study with regard to its readiness to accept your technology?				✓		
4	Have you identified alternative potential markets that you could target as a fall-back position or at a later stage?					✓	
5	Is your core team ready and committed to the success of the venture?						✓
6	Have you identified various scenaria for market entry and worked out a market strategy for each of them?						✓
7	Have you secured enough funds to carry you over the initial period until break-even?				✓		
8	Have you secured critical collaborations with scientific and technological supporting teams?					✓	
9	Have you identified the core suppliers for your raw materials, critical machinery, etc.?						✓
10	Have you identified marketing routes and distribution channels for your product or technology?					✓	
Number of ticks in each column (N)		0	0	0	2	5	3
Weighted totals of each column ($N \times$ column score)		0	0	0	2	10	9
Commercialisation Readiness Index (sum of weighted totals/number of questions) CRI						2.1	

The final CRI score has now improved substantially, reaching 2.1 which showed that she could now initiate steps for commercialisation, carefully, while still continuing to improve here market study (Q3) and trying to attract further funding (Q7). I'm happy to report that the company she sets up a year later is still healthy having succeeded to grow even through the covid19 global health emergency during 2020–2022.

I should emphasise that the list of questions in Table 23.1 is not an exhaustive list since some technologies and products will not fit this scheme perfectly. The exercise, however, will give you a good indication of how well prepared you are to commercialise your technology or product. According to the nature of your technology, you may choose to skip some questions, think of more questions to ask yourself, or change the questions above for a better fit (you may need to adjust your calculations accordingly) in order to get a more reliable CRI.

But the work of an entrepreneur is never done. Once your start-up company is up and running, you should continue all the activities listed above in order to maintain a high Commercialisation Readiness Index at all times. For an enterprise to remain successful after the initial consolidation period, it has to continuously stay in touch with its markets and be aware of the changing needs of its customers. For example, as we discussed before, markets often shift and you should be aware of trends and fads to be ready for them and take advantage of them as they emerge.

The exercise above is not only useful when you are setting up your start-up or spin-off company. Even diversification of activities of a successful company requires exhaustive preparation before it can take the plunge into different markets. Expansion into new markets and new applications is often the secret behind continuing entrepreneurial success, and such expansion should be seen as the start of a whole new venture which requires the same diligent preparation as the setting up of a new start-up company.

In fact, if you decide to diversify your product line or target new markets, you should make sure that your core activities (core focus of your company) are completely steady and solid before pursuing diversification. The only exception to this rule is when the original market has shifted and your technology no longer fits the needs of the market. In this case, you are forced to look into alternative markets (see Question 4 in Tables 23.1 and 23.2) where your technology could fit better.

My general advice in this regard is to put all your efforts into making a success of your new enterprise in your chosen core technology and core markets before attempting a new venture through diversification or expansion. To put it differently: sprint ahead in your core business, and at the same time, build gradually your company's strength and financial virility. When you are completely ready and your core business is steady, then by all means look further afield and test other technologies and other products in new or in the same markets.

Having said that, it is not always obvious when a company has reached a "steady state" when it is steaming along comfortably and successfully with little input from you. Accomplishing this desirable state of affairs might happen, but it will take years at the least, and it is more likely that your enterprise may never reach this state. In all cases, you need to be strict with your assessment of the company's development and prospects. Continuous evaluation and assessment will show you whether it's worth continuing or whether you should cut your losses. Emotional attachment to a business venture is important – it helps to see you through the most difficult early periods – but it cannot replace cool-headed assessment and judgement. Preparedness is key, and your entrepreneurial "sprint" should be measured and focused.

In Summary

A simple way to decide whether you are ready for commercialisation is to answer ten questions and calculate a Commercialisation Readiness Index (CRI). The CRI includes all critical systems that need to be ready (or almost ready) before you decide to take the next steps towards commercialisation, i.e. before you set up your start-up.

Obstacles Are Just Challenges 24

Once your new start-up is up and running, life will be as different as you can possibly imagine. Whereas in your lab your main worry was how to improve your technology and how to get its functionality or properties as competitive as possible, in your new role as an entrepreneur you will be inundated with non-technical (and non-scientific) things to do and decisions to take. Even if you do ensure that your company is managed by a professional manager and your team is working well together, it is you who everyone will turn to for advice and problem resolution. Your focus and aims in your enterprise will be continuously challenged by the small but wearisome day-to-day tasks and challenges that – more often than not – must be addressed as a matter of urgency and that cannot be resolved through the systematic and methodical scientific method that you relied upon previously.

And yet, to make a success of your enterprise, your focus and vision must remain clear and sharp. Successful entrepreneurs have found that if they concentrate on what they know best and do it well the "minor things" in their enterprise somehow manage themselves! This is of course an exaggeration, but the implication is that if the company *vision*, mission, and *aims* are always kept in focus, then the company will find its stable operating condition quicker and will better be able to weather problems.

Rest assured that there will be many problems that will have to be faced during the course of an enterprise's lifetime which will make it hard to stay the course and remain focused on your vision. As this is a fact of entrepreneurial life, I have tried to list in Table 24.1 the main challenges that usually cause serious problems during the early lifetime of a start-up company and their general repercussions, both internally and externally. You may want to add more, depending on your particular situation.

Let us take a closer look at these challenges and how they might affect your operations and market presence:

Ineffective Teamwork It is critical that your team learns to work together efficiently and effectively. Even if your team is mainly made up of collaborators with whom you have worked for many years, the stresses and challenges of working in a

Table 24.1 The main sources of operational problems and their main repercussions during the early life of a start-up

#	Challenges and problems	Potential influence on internal company operations	Potential influence on market presence and perceptions
1	Ineffective teamwork	Loss of operational focus, operational inefficiencies, low morale, operational divergences	Minor and indirect, mainly related to weak operational responses to the market
2	Weak management	Loss of operational control, divergent interests, loss of product RD focus	Weak market perception, slow responses to market needs
3	Insufficient market watch	Incorrect product focus, time and money wastage	Incorrect products, wrong market focus, market losses
4	Insecure funding	Weak RD, product delays, problems in production, marketing, staffing	Weak market presence, narrow marketing range, narrow product range
5	Untimely disclosures	Loss of competitiveness, loss of novelty, RD compromised	Product confusion, loss of market share
6	Unsatisfactory technology cost-benefit ratio	Delays in market entry, weak funding capability, loss of morale, weak returns	Weak market competitiveness, loss of market share, weak perception
7	Ineffective marketing strategy	Weak financial returns, insufficient feedback, loss of focus	Weak market presence, low competitiveness, low market share, market confusion

company – which usually require different skills and capabilities – will test their endurance and abilities. A good professional manager will be able to resolve most issues, but many of the challenges will have to be faced and resolved by you. Some of the trickiest challenges you might face are the personal conflicts which can seemingly arise out of nowhere. Once, I was asked by two young researchers to help them set up a spin-off company based on their doctoral and post-doc work. On speaking to them, I found them to be both very ambitious and driven. The problem, however, was that both had worked on the same topic at different periods from different viewpoints so both had strong but differing opinions with respect to how the spin-off should be directed and what they should aim at. I actually observed this conflict during our second meeting and realised that there was a real danger of them splitting their collaboration if they tried to work together. Suffice to say there is no question that a healthy spin-off could arise from such a situation of significant conflict. My advice to them was first to clarify each other's strengths and only then join forces to form a company.

Weak Management Adapting to a business environment is also very challenging, especially for the founders of a spin-off company who attempt to manage it in parallel. I remember the case of a very able young scientist who was keen to start a spin-off and learn the ropes as an entrepreneur. The problem was that he was excellent as a researcher but not focused or organised enough for business. It took some time before he could accept that not everyone is cut out to be a manager of people and that it's a lot easier to do research than to balance all the ins and outs of running a company. Thankfully, he is still going strong and his small industrial software company – now with a professional manager at the helm – is looking healthy, a full 6 years after its first steps.

Insufficient Market Watching Watching, following, and responding to the market, as discussed previously, is a lot easier said than done. We hardly ever have all the information at our disposal with which to make fully informed decisions and often we have to control our own over-eagerness to follow our "gut feeling" instead of the needs of the market. This is where cold assessment and judgement are critical. Correct information is always a quid pro quo of correct decisions. Also, markets can change very quickly and so should you, all the while keeping your eye on the ball. Monitor your progress and correct your course in good time!

Insecure Funding Finances are going to challenge you sooner or later. There is always an unpleasant feeling of "Where did all the money go?", especially at the beginning. Even if you try to keep strictly within the constraints of your business plan, unforeseen expenses and rising costs will always challenge you. When it comes to finances, things can get out of hand very quickly!

Fresh funding will almost always be necessary to keep the company running until the first income starts appearing. And this is almost always later than planned. My best advice is to get as much funding as you need (according to your business plan) plus a bit more, but not too much more. Having too much money leads to waste and confusion and can easily detract from your business aims. Too many funding sources also add to your own pressures and responsibilities (reporting, justifying, etc.), detracting you even more. Keep your funding options open but only use them when necessary.

Untimely Disclosures The next source of business headaches is confidentiality and the danger of disclosures before you are ready to reach the market. This is such a pertinent issue for new technologies that companies take steps to ensure that their staff are in full knowledge of the dangers of untimely disclosures and their responsibilities thereof via strict NDAs (Non-Disclosure Agreements). Because of the competitive nature of advanced technologies, it is critical to keep the competitive edge of your technology secret until you are ready to market it. This is particularly important in the case of technologies that are difficult to patent, e.g. when their competitiveness depends on a more or less simple innovative adaptation. If it is "simple" (as an innovation often appears in retrospect), it might also be seen as "obvious" (non-obviousness is one of the three main criteria for a successful patent, the others being novelty and utility), hence not patentable or protectable since it would be very difficult to prove any infringement one way or another.

Unsatisfactory Cost-Benefit Ratio The next challenge is one that you, as a researcher, should be best placed to deal with: the techno-economic competitiveness of your technology. The problem here is that, as a technologist, your overriding focus has very likely been to improve your technology's performance and functionality with scant regard for the cost. Only once you start considering market needs will the cost-benefit ratio (i.e. market viability) start becoming more focused. Until this reaches competitive levels to enable market entry, you will be hard pressed to find solutions. Once your market competitiveness is high, you can start considering means and routes for market entry.

Ineffective Marketing Strategy Finally, a major challenge is the development of an effective marketing strategy. Marketing is your "shop window" to the market, and a weak or ineffective strategy can make or break any enterprise. Get it right from the beginning and your efforts will be much easier and the returns much quicker.

A marketing campaign should be both informative and convincing. Accordingly, these should be the aims of your marketing strategy. First, select the right channels. A B2B technology (for new materials, embedded sensors, processes, methods, and so on, i.e. most of the things that lab researchers usually develop) is best served within your networks and by industry magazines and newsletters. Every industrial field has its specialist magazines, usually one or more in each region, some with a global reach. Online industrial magazines are becoming more and more popular so search for and find the ones that are relevant to you and endeavour to publish a short introductory article about your technology. On the other hand, marketing drives for products or services aimed directly at the market will have to concentrate on popular magazines read by users. For example, there is a multitude of software magazines (paper and online) which serve this sector, many of which are highly specialised. In addition, all types of technologies can gain additional traction by being offered in online marketplaces with a careful keyword listing.

Even though all of the above challenges are internal to the start-up, their repercussions can be far-reaching and serious. In all of the cases described above, the overarching considerations that one is called upon to address are the smooth and efficient running of the company and the response of the market to these problems. Of these, it is the market response – and the company's own answer to it – that can have the most damaging and long-lasting effect because it is also the most difficult to deal with and influence. Indeed, it is not just the response of the market to the company but the market's *perception* of the company's operations and its long-term prospects that can prove the most challenging to address.

The market's perception is directly linked with that most important asset of any business: *trust* – both by the market and by funding entities. A high level of trust – and a strong perception of trustworthiness – translates into low risk which improves both your income and funding prospects. As a respected researcher, you are probably starting your entrepreneurial life from a position of high trustworthiness, which is something which you should capitalise upon to establish healthy business relations from the word go. And of course, the better your business relations, the easier will be your resolution of any obstacles you encounter.

In Summary

There will be many problems that will have to be faced during the course of an enterprise's lifetime which will make it hard to stay the course and remain focused on your vision. Some challenges are internal – are caused and can be addressed by making changes – whereas others are external which means that you might be required to change course. The silver lining is that nearly all problems, if identified early enough, can be corrected and by doing so the enterprise and your operations will be optimised too.

There Is Always That Little Bit Extra You Can Offer   25

By the time we decide to set up a start-up company for the purpose of commercialising a technology, we have more or less settled on the application and sector we are aiming at. And so it should be, as this gives a clear focus and direction for our business activities. But a company hardly ever succeeds by concentrating only on one product in one market. Apart from limiting your company's potential, this increases the business risk since so many things can go wrong. Perhaps, our new product is not as competitive as needed to break into a market (especially if there are other products in the same market serving similar needs), or the market shifts or even disappears, or the novelty of the new product is overtaken by new technologies, and so on. The point here is that you should accept early on that to stick to just one product is risky. You should plan as soon as possible alternative products which are based on your technology and aimed at different applications, even in different sectors. These "spill-over" products (or processes, services, etc.) will not only increase your bottom line but will act as safety nets in case your main product should falter. In fact, many such "second thought" or fall-back technologies have gone on to become even more successful than the original product of a company. Interestingly, there are quite a few instances where such spill-over applications have actually been discovered by accident, often by just observing the performance of existing technologies, indicating the large undiscovered potential still existing in many everyday products and processes.

Many very successful modern technologies started life quite modestly in a limited area. Initially, the Internet was simply a way to share data between scientists at CERN, but it grew astronomically when it was realised that such instant communication capability is what people and businesses desperately need. Many other examples exist of this serendipitous "spill-over" effect: the ubiquitous coke drink was originally marketed as a sedative; nylon – invented by a lab accident – was originally aimed only as an industrial material before it became additionally valuable for hosiery and numerous non-industrial uses; certain industrial pigments are also excellent industrial catalysts; the microwave oven is a side application of radar (with much larger market value); the powerful "super glue" is used in eye and other

© The Author(s), under exclusive license to Springer Nature Switzerland AG 2023
G. Vekinis, *The Researcher Entrepreneur*, Management for Professionals,
https://doi.org/10.1007/978-3-031-44358-9_25

surgery where it is impossible to connect soft tissue otherwise; computational fluid dynamics – a very advanced engineering field – is applied very successfully in computer games for amazingly life-like effects; the powerful and now ubiquitous new LEDs are a very valuable commercial application of hitherto rather esoteric semiconducting materials; the special no-glare coatings on spectacle lenses were originally developed for space mirrors; artificial intelligence programmes started life as "expert systems" to answer simple queries before expanding into the impressive supporting systems of today.. the list is endless.

In nearly all cases where a technology expanded from its original – usually successful – application to another one, it happened more or less by a serendipitous accident or by trial and error. This, however, is not always the case: many generic technologies such as materials, sensors, and software algorithms have naturally found applications in many different fields because of their inherently functional versatility. Tungsten carbide was originally developed a hundred years ago as the main constituent of ultra-hard cutting tools for metal working (to this day "Wedia" remains the mainstay of most metal cutting operations), but its excellent mechanical properties have allowed it to be used very successfully in high power ammunition and diamond-producing anvils. Silicon carbide was developed and is still the material of choice for hard sandpaper, but it is also an excellent material for high temperature furnaces and, lately, high temperature electronics which are crucial for space exploration and elsewhere. Nitrous oxide was originally (in the nineteenth century) sold for recreational use (creating euphoria and stimulating laughter), but it is also an excellent anaesthetic during surgery. In a different field, the Monte Carlo numerical algorithm was originally developed as a statistical tool but is now used in numerous fields from engineering design to simulations in physics and chemistry. Many other examples can be found just by looking around and considering the various products used in your everyday life. In fact, you'll be surprised by how many opportunities you can think of for using familiar products in different applications. The same is true with your technology: why stick just to the main use? If you can go a mile with it, think outside the box and go two miles!

Finding alternative applications for your technology doesn't have to be a complete stab in the dark. Apart from the obvious – more or less – route of exploiting its properties in other similar applications, there is a systematic method by which we can unearth "hidden" spill-over applications of a technology in other fields or sectors which are anything but obvious. This can be referred to as a *"functional convergence analysis"*: essentially an adapted SWOT analysis which gradually shifts through many possibilities to arrive at the most promising set of alternative opportunities for the application of your technology.

The underlying idea of "functional convergence analysis" is that the best opportunities for an alternative application of your technology will be those that require the same functionalities as those offered by your technology. Essentially, the basic premise is that *if some diverse applications share common functionality and properties, it may be possible to satisfy them both using the same technology*. In the case of materials, a whole new methodology has arisen based on the same principle, entitled "Materials Selection", which uses a similar approach (Fig. 25.1).

25 There Is Always That Little Bit Extra You Can Offer

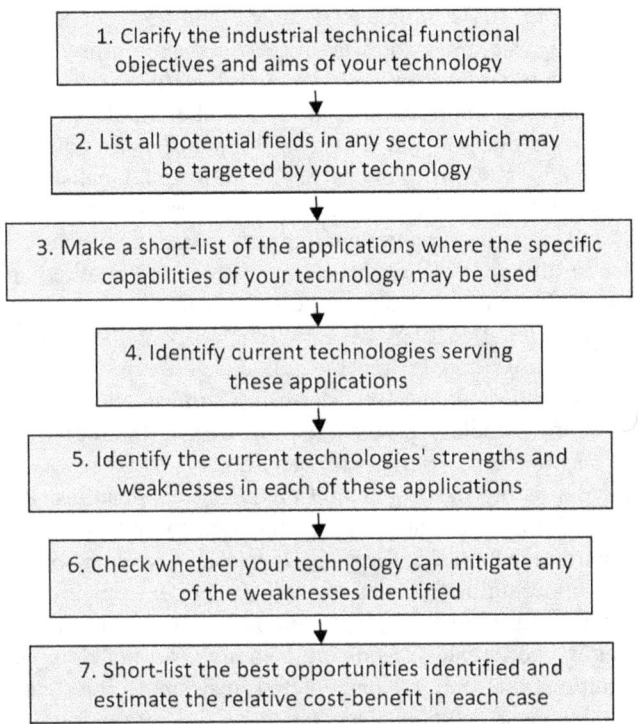

Fig. 25.1 Functional convergence analysis to identify potential alternative areas of application of your technology

In more detail, the various steps for carrying out "functional convergence analysis" are as follows:

1. Clarify the functional objectives and aims of your technology, i.e. what it offers to industry or the market. These should be considered from the point of view of the users since most probably they are not the same as the scientific and technical objectives. For example, a miniature micro-electro-mechanical (MEM) high power frequency modulator is aimed at being embedded in a communication device to improve its performance or functionality in various terrestrial or space applications. A new numerical algorithm for ultra-fast fluid dynamics simulations may be aimed for engineering design of new turbomachinery but also for air-current mixing calculations in meteorology. A new nanostructured coating process may be used to produce either hard, protective layers or coatings with catalytic or aesthetic functions in applications where the existing solutions, if any, are unsatisfactory. In fact, in this second example, the process and the resulting coatings are separate technologies which can be targeted independently.
2, 3. The next step is to draw up a list of all potential fields in any sector that could possibly benefit from what your technology is offering. Continuing with the

examples above, an MEM miniature module could be successfully used in any application where system size and weight needs to be minimised. Possible sectors (and corresponding applications) that could benefit are aerospace (position transponders), medical (embedded in situ diagnostic microsystems and medicine delivery actuators), transport and security (GPS monitors for containers, vehicles, pets), satellite-feed systems (remote exploration and localising), and others. Ultra-fast CFD code is used in mechanical engineering (turbine design, pumps, valves, etc.), but realistic computer gaming can benefit directly as can heart-valve development in the medical field. Hard nanostructured coatings are utilised in high-value mechanical engineering applications where surface wear is a problem while similar functional coatings with catalytic properties can be used for environmental protection (conversion of emitted gases in industry or vehicle exhausts), health and medicine (self-sterilising surfaces, needles, utensils, etc.), space exploration (planetary protection from earthly microbial contamination, self-sterilising astronaut quarters), and many others.

4. Once you have a listing of all potential fields and applications, find out all the methods and technologies that are currently used to address them, if any, and whether the current technologies serving them are satisfactory or not – these last ones represent opportunities for your technology. For example, find out what kind of transponders are used for space exploration and whether they are satisfactory in each application, i.e. small yet powerful enough, accurate, reliable under all possible conditions that may be encountered, resistant to interference, etc. This step will be the most difficult since much of the information is not readily available and will require extensive research. Do this for all potential applications identified and draw up a ranked list of current technologies with those offering the most potential at the top. In fact, at the top of the list, you might list applications where there are currently no solutions available! These are exactly the applications you should concentrate on right from the outset. On the other hand, the bottom of the list will show you which applications you should not bother with. These applications are already well served and your own technology will not farewell if you attempt entry.

When compiling the list of most promising candidate applications for your technology, remember also to include applications where there are solutions but which are of limited availability due to some – usually strategic – restriction, geographic, or other. A case in point is the many space technologies that have been developed as part of the US space efforts and so are only available in the USA and restricted for use elsewhere under the ITAR (International Traffic in Arms Regulations) rules. These rules are so wide-ranging that a large number of electronics, thermal, and other systems are restricted (even though they would not appear to fall under the "Arms" designation) outside the USA, thereby opening up a plethora of opportunities in Europe and elsewhere for new substitute technologies. Similar restrictions exist in France and elsewhere for dual use strategic technologies.

Similar sources of opportunities are provided by the European Union's decision to attempt to become more technologically independent of other countries in a large number of industrial areas in an effort to safeguard European manufacturing industry and markets from fluctuations in cost and in the availability of some critical technologies (e.g. China tried to restrict the export of many critical rare-earth materials a few years ago, although it has since relaxed that position, on the basis of them becoming scarcer). The main beneficiaries in technological sectors in this case have been advanced materials, electronics, and energy technologies as well as some medical and paramedical fields.

5. The next step is to carry out a detailed SWOT analysis of the existing technologies' strengths and weaknesses in each of these applications so you can identify those applications that are currently unfulfilled by any existing technologies. This is where you'll concentrate your efforts. On the other hand, those applications (in any sector) which are already well satisfied (as evidenced by particular strengths of the current technology) should be avoided as non-fertile grounds for a new technology. In this regard, those applications (by particular users) that have recently been fulfilled by any technology should also be avoided as it would be difficult to convince a user to adopt yet another new technology for the same application.

6, 7. Once you have your short-list of most promising applications – the top few in the list of all potential applications – you need to carry out a careful analysis of the advantages and disadvantages that your technology may confer on each of these applications. Again, be aware that users often look for different things than we do in our own technology, techno-economic *viability* being paramount in their considerations. In fact, anything to do with costs – direct, such as cost-benefit, or indirect, such as any disruption in production – is always taken into consideration when a decision to adopt a technology is being made. Other critical aspects in this regard are compatibility with other technologies and exploitation capability of the potential users, i.e. skills level available, financial capability, etc.

In conclusion, it is worth reiterating that the value of a technology is directly dependent on the need or demand expressed by the industry and market it is aimed at. The more such industries and markets you can find for your technology – and the more dissatisfied these markets are with existing technologies – the more valuable your enterprise will be. By identifying new opportunities and developing your technologies to satisfy them, you will add significant value to your technology and especially your start-up.

In Summary

A start-up company is set up for the purpose of commercialising a technology so it has to be tightly focused on that purpose. But a company hardly ever succeeds by concentrating only on one product in one market. Ideally one should early on look for spill-over opportunities and develop alternative products based on the same technology but aimed at different applications, even in different sectors. Functional convergence analysis helps in deciding.

Consolidate First, Diversify Later

26

Have you ever found yourself, as a researcher developing a new technology, in two – or more – minds about which application you should target first as you move towards commercialisation? You are not alone in this – it is the nature of any new, highly promising technology to offer many commercialisation directions, each of them exciting and promising of success.

There is no doubt that the decision regarding which application you should aim for first – toward which you will devote all your early commercialisation efforts and funds – will be critical for the success of your start-up enterprise. In fact, the foundations of your company should be closely anchored to this particular application (or closely related applications) before you consider diversification later on into new applications and markets.

This much is recognised and accepted, but how exactly do you go about deciding which first-targeted application will give you the best chance of early consolidation in the market? This is a major decision since all your early efforts and funds for your start-up will have to be aimed in that direction, and a complete change in direction will be very difficult or even impossible during the early stages.

Deciding on which application you should aim for first is not an easy task as you want to ensure that you offer something that the market or industry needs or wants but at the same time avoid jumping in a crowded pool full of existing solutions. The trick, therefore, is to find the application or applications – and sector – where your technology will have maximum effectiveness *and* is needed, even if it is not the largest or most obvious market for your technology. In other words, you must look for an application to target where your technology will be proven and become well known and successful and only *then* will you be able to ride this wave of success into a larger and more crowded market. It is the successful debut of your technology in an appropriate application and sector that will pave the way to wider success later.

This strategy may at first appear contradictory to what we discussed earlier, about allowing the market to guide you to the most optimum application. It is not a contradiction for the following reason: while the market always remains your guide, you must approach your optimum market goal in a more round-about, indirect way. If you jump directly into the fray in a large, crowded market, your competitors will try to cut you down in many ways. They may undercut your efforts, spread rumours, or invoke customer loyalty in an – often unfair – attempt to dissuade any industry from even testing your technology. They may even threaten to withdraw their supplies from your distributors or customers if they so much allow your new technology any breathing space. These are all unfair business practices, but unfortunately, they happen all the time.

It goes without saying that if your technology does not have any competition, then you won't need such a round-about way – you should aim straight for the largest and most promising market where the need is greatest. Unfortunately, not only is this situation very rare, but it is also risky as a strategy since it depends wholly on the availability of completely reliable information and a very accurate market and technology watch. Remember that many embedded technologies are not visible (e.g. control software, sensors, special materials, special production processes, etc.) so you can never be 100% sure of what's inside a black box.

Be that as it may, the strategy recommended above has its own pitfalls. The market you choose for your debut may *appear* to offer minimum competition in your technology's area for other reasons. It may be too restrictive and highly standardised – for example, space or military – to easily allow a newcomer leeway to prove a new technology. Or it may be too small to allow operating space for another viable enterprise, as often happens in the space industry. Or it may be served by technologies exclusively produced internally by the end users, e.g. for maximum security and confidentiality. All of these things can be ascertained by a careful market analysis, and it is useful to be aware of them before you commit yourself to such a move.

A Market-Prioritisation Decision Matrix

So how do you go about deciding which could be a promising debut market to enter first with your new enterprise? Bear in mind that you should always keep your options open, as it might very well transpire that the largest market may well be the most promising for your technology after all, even if competition exists in that market.

There are many detailed criteria you could consider for making the selection, but most are interrelated while 11 of these are more or less distinct. It also helps to carry out this decision exercise using a simple scoring system and then adding up your scores, as in your CRI calculation. Table 26.1 shows a typical result of this exercise using a scoring system of 0–5 to indicate the relative merits of a technology over existing solutions.

Considering the underlying meanings of the criteria in Table 26.1, one can see that the first four (#1, #2, #3 and #4) refer to the relative *fitness for purpose* of your technology in the particular application and market. In other words, they are a measure of how much more fit your technology is in that market vis-à-vis other potential or existing solutions. Another four criteria (#6, #7, #9 and #10) refer to the

A Market-Prioritisation Decision Matrix

Table 26.1 A scoring system for deciding the most optimum debut market for your technology. Use zero (0) for "Nothing" and "5" for "Maximum". Scores shown refer to a real case, as discussed in the text

#	Selection criterion	Market A	Market B	Market C	Market D
1	How much added value does your technology offer in this market?	4	1	1	2
2	What is the relative TRL[a] of your technology for this application?	3	1	1	2
3	What is the relative cost/benefit ratio of your technology for this application?	2	3	2	5
4	What is the relative technical competitiveness of your technology in this application/market?	3	2	1	4
5	Do you have effective contacts and collaborations in this market?	1	3	1	4
6	Can you enter this market without further major investments?	2	2	4	4
7	Can you avoid any vested interests or well entrenched technologies serving this application?	2	4	2	4
8	Do you have prior experience in this market?	3	1	5	2
9	Can you obtain rapid responses in this market?	2	3	1	4
10	What is the level of need of this market for your technology?	2	3	3	4
11	What are the future prospects of this market?	3	2	2	3
	Totals	27	25	23	38

[a]Technology Readiness Level, see the TT Guide

market in relation to your technology, while #5 and #8 refer to your own experience in this market and #11 refers to the health and future prospects of this market, irrespective of your technology. Naturally, other criteria are also possible, and you should consider your own situation carefully to see if you should include other criteria for completeness.

The scores shown in Table 26.1 are drawn from a real-life exercise carried out for a new thermally sprayed hard coating on a softer metallic substrate. The clearly "winning" market ("Market D") is a specialist segment of the printing industry with very strong prospects. The other markets, all of which were large, were segments of the automotive and transport industries. Although their scores are not low either, the safe bet for this start-up would be to enter the printing industry first, prove and consolidate the capabilities of their technology there, and then attempt to move to the large mass markets.

Once you have proven and consolidated your technology, you will be in a much better position to convince other users of its capabilities and increase the portfolio of your enterprise. In fact, you will also be in a much better position to identify new uses and start planning for entering new markets, perhaps in completely new sectors – namely, you will be ready to diversify. This happens very often in the case of new high-performance materials, both functional and structural, which need to prove their worth in a challenging environment first before being widely accepted. An excellent case in point is the very wide range of uses that carbon fibre-reinforced polymer (CFRP) composites have found over the past 30 or so years in many sectors. While initially CFRP was considered to be a specialist material too expensive for everyday use (it was originally developed for military and in particular so-called "stealth" planes), it is now found in a plethora of retail products from sports goods to cars, boats, and even furniture!

Another good example of a technology that proved itself in one sector and then diversified successfully in many others is the laser. While originally it was mainly used as a tool in physics labs, it is now ubiquitous in DVD readers and writers, pointers, toys, engineering instruments, and many military and scientific applications. It has even spawned the huge optoelectronics industry and is now promising to revolutionise data transfer by offering incredible data transfer rates between computers with very low heating, a crucial consideration for large data centres.

The now ubiquitous GPS (Global Positioning System) was once a secret development for military purposes, but it is now in a multitude of commercial and personal applications from finding an address to tracking a container and even finding your car if it is stolen or mislaid. Motion sensors used to be mainly industrial tools, but they are now found in cars, security apparatus, and even toys. Finally, induction coils are used in physics laboratories for teaching and in electronics but are now slowly coming into their own as cordless charging stations and miniature heating coils for jewellers and craftsmen.

In conclusion, it is wise to think of your technology's commercialisation development as a step-by-step process where each successive step is built on the foundation provided by the previous, successful, step. Such a "consolidation before diversification" strategy does not preclude parallel development, but it does reduce commercialisation risks, and in particular, it reduces the dangers of facing aggressive competitors before you are strong enough to stand on your own feet.

In Summary

While alternative products are important, the name of your start-up will be made (or lost) by its first important offering, i.e. your core technological product. It is the successful debut of your technology in an appropriate application and sector that will pave the way to wider success later. But which market to focus on is not easy and a "market-prioritisation decision matrix" will help you decide.

Diamonds from Ashes   27

The comic actor (and philosopher on the side) Woody Allen has put it very well: "If you're not failing every now and again, it's a sign you're not doing anything very innovative".

Exactly the same applies to setting up a start-up company to commercialise your innovative technology. "Innovation" by definition means something novel, something not yet attempted. It is possible that, even after all your best efforts and preparations, an innovative product or technology might not catch on and your enterprise ends in failure. But such financial failures are never a waste of time. They are valuable trials that do not succeed for particular reasons and in so doing point the way to a better approach.

There are no better teachers than well understood failures. Hardly ever do you see new approaches and new technologies succeeding that have not had to contend with numerous hitches and failures along the way. It is the failures that teach us the most and pave the way for eventual successes in the long run.

The truth of this becomes evident time and time again in the technology transfer process. An example from my own personal experience may help to illustrate this. When I first teamed up with a professional managing director and launched a spin-off company (based on my research work on microwave heating), we made the mistake of assuming that the large market we had in mind was going to love our technology, given our calculations that it offered tremendous cost savings in production. Little did we realise that, in the eyes of the workers in the factory where it was first installed, our technology represented a direct threat to the survival of their jobs! Although our business and technological preparation was extremely thorough, such extraneous obstacles caused many headaches and additional effort to resolve. This led to serious delays which increased overall risk and financial setbacks. At the end, we did manage to pull through by pulling out of the original installation and concentrating on a different application (without such extraneous obstacles), but the financial damage was long-lasting. The moral of the story is that our eventual success came from learning from and avoiding the mistakes that led to the original failure. In fact, it becomes apparent in hindsight that we could have saved ourselves a lot of the financial damage we suffered if we had *not* persevered as much as we did and had pulled out of the original installation sooner than we eventually did.

Learning from our failures is part of our research life too. It is rare that we know from the start the answers to the research challenges we are addressing; by necessity, we often move in the dark, trying new approaches and new ideas until we find a solution. While prior experiences help to guide us to a great extent, many research projects end in partial or – thankfully rarely – complete failure. It is these failures that give us the necessary insights to focus and hone our search, gradually reaching the solution or the answer to a problem.

Failures are much more frequent in entrepreneurship, not only because of the greater (and usually more financially burdensome) difficulties and challenges involved, but because so many of these problems are extraneous and we usually have very little control over them. As discussed above, the unpredictability of the market means that there is always a risk of failure, for example, if we miss the trend or misread the need. As long as we see such failures as intermediate stops and lessons, with instructive – and constructive – potential, we will eventually reach success. As the saying goes, "if at first you don't succeed, try and try again".

In many advanced industrialised countries, entrepreneurial failure is never seen as a waste. Entrepreneurs – and researchers – are encouraged and supported in their attempts at commercialisation of their inventions – generally by setting up a start-up company – even if this ends in failure, because the governments know that such support (and such failures) is nothing less than entrepreneurial training. In such countries, government funds will be happy to support you again even if you did not succeed in commercialising your technology the first time. Furthermore, young people are taught from a very early age the principle of "nothing ventured, nothing gained" and encouraged to try to commercialise their ideas even at the beginning of their careers.

This is particularly evident in the USA. In the famous "Silicon Valley" near San Francisco, where many of the modern Internet giants were born, a saying that exactly reflects the get-up-and-go attitude of the local start-up entrepreneurs is "fail fast, fail often!" Students at local universities very often found and lead small enterprises even while studying. While many fail – meaning that the target market or industry impact did not materialise as they had hoped for – they all benefit from the experience and are impatient to try again as soon as the next opportunity presents itself. The long-term benefits of this attitude are recognised by the federal and state governments there which are extremely supportive of any student willing to give entrepreneurship a try.

It is well known that Bill Gates, the founder of Microsoft, made unsuccessful attempts while still a student to commercialise a number of early ideas before finally succeeding with the MS DOS operating system. He freely admits that it was those failures and the lessons he learnt from them that paved the way to his later success. In fact, nearly all of the present large Internet companies found success after a string of failed attempts at various commercialisation ventures.

I cannot emphasise enough that a failure at commercialisation of a well-developed technology is never the opposite of success in the market. A commercialisation failure is only a *stepping stone* to success – an intermediate stage of testing new ideas and approaches on the way to eventual financial or societal achievement. In some cases, the gap is small: a change in direction towards a new application or sector may bring success. In other cases, the problem is more intricate and might involve technological change to meet higher or different market expectations, for example. In most cases, commercialisation of viable and well-developed technologies is only a matter of correct timing, of taking advantage of an opportunity, and always of sufficient patience and perseverance.

Technology commercialisation setbacks or failures can result from many situations, extraneous or internal. How we deal with each situation depends on each particular case, but we can identify a number of reasons for failure and appropriate responses thereto. In Table 27.1, I have listed many of the most common, mainly market-related reasons for failure of a commercialisation attempt (relevant mainly to start-ups, but the reasons are valid for any type of commercialisation route) and included suggestions for appropriate responses. The table does not include every reason for commercialisation failure – for example, it does not include internal operational or financial problems which you would most likely be best placed to identify and resolve – but it is meant as a guide to help you derive benefit from mainly extraneous setbacks and failures.

I should emphasise that in preparing Table 27.1, I have assumed that you have completed all stages of your technology preparation according to Fig. 1.1 and Table 5.1 of the TT Guide and that you have reached at least Stage 8 (or Stage 6 for the last three reasons in Table 27.1), ready for market entry. If you have not achieved at least Stage 8 (or Stage 6 for the last three rows in Table 27.1), then failure should be expected, and the suggested responses will not be much use to you at this point.

To use the table, first identify the main cause of failure of your start-up (or other commercialisation route) and then consider how to adapt one or more of the suggested responses for your particular case before you attempt to commercialise your technology again.

As with every activity related to commercialisation, there is no guarantee that the suggested responses will offer a viable and long-term solution and allow your enterprise to succeed. Whether the reason or reasons for failure are extrinsic – i.e. market related – or intrinsic, your job is to minimise their effects and try to build a defence strategy against them or shift your direction in order to avoid them.

In all cases, it is crucial to remember that nearly all technology commercialisation successes were the end result of a sequence or cascade of attempts, each of which provided a little more knowledge and experience to provide surer foundations for the next. It is this gradual process and perseverance on your part – the entrepreneurial "try and try again" – that will lead to eventual success. Or as has been said in a half joking and half serious vein: "to succeed, all you need to do is get up one oftener than you fall down".

Table 27.1 Common reasons for failure of a technology commercialisation attempt and possible responses for remediation

#	Main cause of failure of commercialisation	Suggested remediation responses
1	Target market or industry not ready for your technology or economic downturn reduces demand	• Change target market to one that is ready for your technology • Reconsider commercialisation timing to coincide with new regulations, improved economy or public wishes or demands • Adapt technology closer to market needs and capabilities to use it
2	Target market or industry saturated by existing technologies	• Choose target market that is closer to your technology's strengths • Improve your technology's cost or cost/benefit ratio
3	The market or industry does not know of your technology	• Expand briefing and marketing strategy to more sectors • Publish "briefing" papers in industry journals
4	Target market or industry unwilling to test your technology	• Offer more free evaluation installations in key markets • Take steps to improve public perception of your technology • Increase your marketing and exposure efforts • Choose market or industry with greater need for your technology
5	Market has shifted away (trend has dissipated)	• Adapt your technology to follow the market shift • Change target market or sector to one that is more compatible
6	A new technology poses a threat during your own market entry	• Change to a market closer to your technology's main strengths • Focus marketing on your main strengths
7	Existing market players employing unfair practices to deny you market entry	• Consider legal means to fight unfair competition • Concentrate on markets that other players are not interested in until you consolidate your position and reputation
8	Cost or cost/benefit ratio too high for the target industry or market	• Update your market research • Carry out a cost analysis of your technology to reduce production costs • Change target market or sector to one that is more compatible
9	Pilot or industrial tests are very expensive	• Apply for post-TRL6 funding to test your technology in industry • Consider joint development with large potential user • Stagger the development costs over many stages • Carry out cost analysis to reduce costs

(continued)

Table 27.1 (continued)

#	Main cause of failure of commercialisation	Suggested remediation responses
10	Pilot or industrial tests are inconclusive	• Improve performance and/or cost/benefit ratio • Change target industry to one closer to your technology's strengths • Repeat tests with different parameters

In Summary

It is possible that, even after all your best efforts and preparations, an innovative product or technology might not catch on and your enterprise ends in failure. But such financial failures are never a waste of time. They are valuable trials that do not succeed for particular reasons and in so doing point the way to a better approach. Failures are chances to learn lessons to point the way to eventual success. Every successful entrepreneur has failed – often more than once – on the way to success.

Open a Window to the World   28

As researchers, one of the ways in which we are judged and evaluated is by the number of "citations", i.e. the level of interest shown by our peers all over the world in our published reports and patents as indicated by their referencing of our work. Whether you agree with this parameter or not – personally I think it can be very misleading – it illustrates a very important point: if you don't publish or present your work publicly, it will remain unknown and unevaluated and your name along with it. In fact, the best way to prove ownership of a technology or know-how is via a publication or patent. One might say that via our publications we open a window so that the world can look at our work.

Indeed, the need to expose our work to scrutiny goes much further than that. Over the last 20 or so years, research projects in Europe (as well as in most industrialised countries worldwide) are being carried out by consortia of partners from universities, research centres, and private companies. To be included in such consortia, we sometimes resort to "advertising" our know-how and expertise in databases through "expressions of interest". In other words, we *market* ourselves and our laboratories to be able to join consortia and compete for research contracts.

The critical need for effective marketing [1] of one's technology and know-how should therefore not be surprising for a researcher who wishes to become an entrepreneur. The necessity to maximise the dissemination of the capabilities of your technology is of paramount importance to enable success in entrepreneurship. First of all, the *existence* of your technology needs to be made known and publicised right at the start of your decision to commercialise. As a new technology, potential customers and users must first be made aware of its presence in the pool of potential technologies addressing a challenge. At the same time, you need to clarify the unique aspects of your technology vis-à-vis other solutions that may already exist and discuss rigorously the advantages and disadvantages of each solution.

---

[1] "Marketing" here is used in the narrow sense of informing the market and disseminating the technology's capabilities and utility.

Table 28.1 Suggested technology information dissemination channels according to type of technology

Target	Type of technology	Primary info. dissemination channel	Secondary info. dissemination channel
Industry (B2B)	Material	Industry journal	Scientific/technological publication
	Device, system	Industry journal	Demonstration/evaluation installation
	Method, protocol	Customised presentation	Industry journal
	Software	Demonstration/evaluation installation	Industry journal
	Process	Industry journal	Fairs and exhibitions, customised presentation
	Service	Industry journal	Customised presentation
Direct to market	Material	Scientific/technological publication	Direct advertising
	Device, system	Direct advertising	Fairs and exhibitions
	Software	Demonstration/evaluation installation	Customised presentation
	Service	Direct advertising	Customised presentation

The way you go about making your technology known to potential customers, i.e. advertising your technology and disseminating critical information about it, depends on its nature and whether it is aimed directly at the market (i.e. supplied directly to end users) or at industry to be used to produce something else (B2B, discussed earlier). In all cases, your aim is to maximise knowledge about your product or technology, especially in relation to other technologies.

As there are many ways to disseminate information, you will have to determine which will be the best for you. As always, the optimum methods depend on the type of technology you have developed and Table 28.1 presents a simple matrix for deciding on the most promising channels.

In all cases, you must keep in mind that the most effective way to disseminate information about your new technology and announce your decision to commercialise it via a start-up or otherwise is via your network of scientific and business contacts, especially entities that you have collaborated with in the past and who know and trust you. As discussed before, trust is one of the main pillars of any successful business and you will have a much better chance of being listened to by scientific or business collaborators than by unknown entities.

Two main parameters are used to categorise technologies in Table 28.1: whether the technology is targeted as B2B or directly to users; and the type of technology, i.e. whether it is a device, material, service, and so on. The information dissemination methods that are suggested include direct advertising, industry journals, customised presentations, fairs and exhibitions, scientific or technological publications, demonstrations and evaluation installations, and more. Combinations of these are also possible and often desirable.

Note that in Table 28.1, methods, protocols, and processes are not included under the "direct to market" target since these technologies are not generally offered directly to consumers in the market.

Note also that "direct advertising" includes all modes and channels used to reach customers directly, including all types of paper and electronic media.

A particular technology may fall under more than one category and therefore be amenable to various dissemination channels. For example, a new sensor may either be embedded in a system made by another industry or packaged as a stand-alone product and marketed directly to the market (e.g. an electronic thermometer).

Another important point is that different target markets and industries for the same technology (appropriately adapted) may force you to deploy different dissemination approaches. For example, a new joining process for a carbon-fibre light-weight structure for a space application will benefit more from a customised presentation to the end user while the same process for a mass production industry will probably benefit more from a publication in an industry journal in the form of a "Technology Brief".

Industrial journal publications are an excellent mode of B2B advertising of new technologies. Most high-quality industry (or "trade") journals publish technological short papers where you can expound on the principles of operation and utility of your technology and present case studies. In the same journals, you can also publish shorter "technology briefs" which give an informative snapshot of the new technology and its merits.

Specialised fairs, exhibitions, and demonstrations at industrial conferences are always very good fora for introducing appropriate new technologies since you will be addressing a receptive audience that has a clear interest in the potential applications of your technology.

Last but certainly not least, all new technologies require industrial "test beds", that is, industrial field demonstrations and evaluation installations which are extremely important because they will help you to field-test your technology under completely realistic conditions and at the same time help to advertise your technology's capabilities. Such field-tests should be completed during development Stage 7 (see TT Guide), but any additional industrial field installations can give new complementary information, and you can also use them as demonstrations for prospective customers to visit.

In Summary

The necessity to maximise the dissemination of the capabilities of your technology is of paramount importance to enable success in entrepreneurship. First of all, the *existence* of your technology needs to be made known and publicised right at the start of your decision to commercialise, and at the same time, you need to clarify the unique aspects of your technology vis-à-vis other solutions that may already exist and discuss rigorously the advantages and disadvantages of each solution.

A Final Thought: Proactivity Beats Reactivity Every Time

29

So, you have taken the major decision to step out of your lab and become an entrepreneur! You have led and guided your new technology to TRL8, and it is now a highly promising and innovative product or service which you are about to offer to industry or to the market as a newly fledged entrepreneur. In the process, you have taken all possible steps and safeguards to maximise your enterprise's chance of success.

And now for the million-dollar question: assuming you do carry out all that's expected from you, is there a guarantee that success will come your way?

Unfortunately, there is not. Whether an enterprise will be successful or not is *indeterminate*. There is no way of knowing what will happen tomorrow in your chosen market and whether some new, unknown factor will suddenly come into play and affect the chances of your enterprise succeeding. There are many factors that are completely out of our control and which can easily make the difference between success and failure. Unforeseen worsening of the general economic climate or a sudden change in a market trend you have been following or a change in perception as regards your technology by your customers can all have a very serious effect on your business. The best defence you can use in such cases is to deal with the situation as soon as possible and go along with it *until* you have made all the necessary changes and improvements to your production or business process that will allow you to survive and prosper once again.

And this is the point. Although the actual future of your company is *indeterminate*, it is *not uncertain* since you will be continuously monitoring the market and, at the first sign of weakness or trouble, step in and carry out all the changes you can in order to improve your chances of business success. This means you need to have significant flexibility in operations which should therefore always be part of your thinking as an entrepreneur. Every one of your business operations should be monitored on an almost continuous basis and adjusted and optimised as the prevailing conditions dictate. Such an approach is like playing poker with unlimited capability of making corrections to your hand at any time in the game!

The necessity of such flexibility was alluded to at length in the previous chapter, but you certainly should not have to wait until failure is staring you in the face before you decide to make changes and optimise operations. This should be an on-going process and you should aim to have back-up positions for all critical operations or processes.

There are many examples of famous companies that saw the writing on the wall in good time and instituted changes – sometimes momentous changes – to their operations and eventually succeeded. In the late 1990s, the well-known Apple Inc. was fast becoming just a niche company in the computer market even though their quality and technology were always considered to be excellent, even by their competitors. A few years later, by changing their emphasis from computers to high-end, well-designed consumer electronics (nearly all based on their computer expertise), they achieved a huge turnaround and are now among the world's largest companies with very high profitability and excellent reputation. This was the direct result of their capability for flexibility and building upon their reputation without losing touch with their underlying strengths.

The need for flexibility is just as important to a large company as it is for a new start-up. In fact, flexibility of operations is far more important to a new start-up trying to find its feet and forge a position in a competitive market – against many obstacles – than to an existing company that has established itself and is operating successfully. While the latter can weather market storms to some extent by relying on accumulated safety nets (financial, technological, and other), the former can only rely on its speed of response and flexibility to bend with the prevailing wind in order to survive until it too accumulates financial and other safeguards, ready for the next storm.

In our laboratories as researchers, although we don't take the overall decisions, we almost always have some control over our operations, and we can generally set the pace, direction, and processes of our work. Even in industrial laboratories, where we can't usually decide the overall direction of our research, we do have some say regarding the pace and processes we are going to utilise to achieve our objectives. Most of the time, we also have a say as to when and how to change our pace and processes, for example in order to study a new phenomenon or examine a promising new direction. This means that our research is mainly internalised – the objectives are set internally – and we rarely have to worry about any extraneous forces that could impact on our work. Even in those cases when a technology we are developing is overtaken before we have had a chance to publish or patent, all is not lost since we still have the know-how and experience to go one step further.

As entrepreneurs, however, we are dependent on the market. On the one hand, we have the power to make any decisions we wish in the running of our company but, on the other hand, we are always affected by many extraneous factors, most of which we cannot control. As a result, we have to see all our operations as subject to adjustment and revision as a consequence of and in response to changes in external situations. By doing this carefully and wisely on an on-going basis, we are generally able to weather market storms and even come out healthier and stronger, even if it means we need to change markets or directions. The challenge is therefore to foresee and predict such major upheavals and start preparing for them in good time.

It's not always possible to foresee all potentially dangerous market or industry events and situations, but sometimes telltale signs can appear that should make us sit up and take notice. Many of these are actually internalised, e.g. a *sudden* drop in our sales may mean a sudden obstacle in the market for our technology which may be the result of a shift in a trend, upcoming regulatory restriction, a new perception or expectation, a new competitor, new technological competition, etc. It is up to us to investigate and find out what has caused this sudden drop in sales.

On the other hand, a *gradual* decrease in sales may mean that our company's competitiveness is gradually fading and we are no longer providing the solutions needed or demanded by the market, as the market develops. The reasons for this are generally more difficult to establish, but you need to look for evidence of reduced relevance of your products in the market, decline of interest on the part of your normal customers as a result of newer technologies appearing and competing against you for your market share, reduced effectiveness and efficiency of your operations, weak marketing operations, and so on.

All of the above notwithstanding, a successful entrepreneur should therefore not only react to events and problems but also be proactive and prepare for such eventualities that could affect his or her company. And this is where our research experience pays. As researchers, we learn to watch for signs of technological upheavals – positive or negative – so that we can enter the field and make our mark early on by publishing as soon as possible. As a *researcher entrepreneur*, you can and should apply exactly such experiences to your start-up company and prepare your company early on for tackling this new market or opportunity.

And this is the crux of it all: *a Researcher Entrepreneur is already fully equipped and trained to respond effectively to entrepreneurial opportunities and successfully make the transition to the market-centred world.* With sufficient preparation and planning, continuous monitoring, evaluation, and flexibility, you can leverage such experience and expertise in the market to achieve success as an entrepreneur!

In Summary

Although the actual future – success or failure or something in-between – of your company is *indeterminate*, it is *not uncertain* since you know you must continuously monitor the market and, at the first sign of weakness or trouble, step in and carry out all the changes you can in order to improve your chances of business success. Significant flexibility is key in entrepreneurial operations and should therefore always be part of your thinking as an entrepreneur. Proactivity always beats reactivity in business.

I Wish You All the Best of Luck in Your New Venture!

Further Reading

1. "The Oxford Handbook of Entrepreneurship", by Anuradha Basu (ed.), Mark Casson (ed.), Nigel Wadeson (ed.) and Bernard Yeung (ed.), Oxford Academic, 2008
2. "The Economics of Entrepreneurship", by Simon C. Parker, Cambridge University Press, 2009
3. "From the Basement to the Dome: How MIT's Unique Culture Created a Thriving Entrepreneurial Community", by Jean-Jacques Degroof, The MIT Press, 2021
4. "Mastering Technology Transfer: From Invention to Innovation", by George Vekinis, Springer, 2023
5. "Founders, Apply the Scientific Method to Your Startup", by Chiara Spina, Arnaldo Camuffo, and Alfonso Gambardella, Harvard Business Review, 2020. Accessed at https://hbr.org/2020/11/founders-apply-the-scientific-method-to-your-startup
6. "Innovation Doesn't Have to Be Disruptive", by W. Chan Kim and Renée Mauborgne, Harvard Business Review, 2020. Accessed at https://hbr.org/2023/05/innovation-doesnt-have-to-be-disruptive
7. "New Research: The Skills That Make an Entrepreneur", by Bill J. Bonnstetter, Harvard Business Review, 2012. Accessed at https://hbr.org/2012/12/new-research-the-skills-that-m
8. "From Researcher to Entrepreneur: How to Get Out of Your Comfort Zone, One Step at a Time", by Ana Barjasic, London School of Economics, 2020. Accessed at https://blogs.lse.ac.uk/careers/2020/11/30/from-researcher-to-entrepreneur/
9. "What Researchers Who Want to Be Entrepreneurs Need to Know", by Susan R. Morrissey, Chemical & Engineering News, 2012. Accessed at https://cen.acs.org/articles/90/i34/Researchers-Want-Entrepreneurs-Need-Know.html
10. "The Third Way: Becoming an Academic Entrepreneur", by Javier Garcia-Martinez, Science, 2014. Accessed at https://www.science.org/content/article/third-way-becoming-academic-entrepreneur
11. "Technology-Based Nascent Entrepreneurship: Implications for Economic Policymaking", by James A. Cunningham (ed.) and Conor O'Kane (ed.), Palgrave Macmillan, 2017

GPSR Compliance

The European Union's (EU) General Product Safety Regulation (GPSR) is a set of rules that requires consumer products to be safe and our obligations to ensure this.

If you have any concerns about our products, you can contact us on

ProductSafety@springernature.com

In case Publisher is established outside the EU, the EU authorized representative is:

Springer Nature Customer Service Center GmbH
Europaplatz 3
69115 Heidelberg, Germany

www.ingramcontent.com/pod-product-compliance
Lightning Source LLC
LaVergne TN
LVHW021334080526
838202LV00003B/168